NEW SOCIAL ECONOMY DEVELOPMENT

JOHN LOK

ISBN 979-888591478-9

Contents

Foreword

Introduction

What is our social new economic measurement method ? The objective of macroeconomic behavioral methods is to control the short run behavior of an country's economy development. Is it useful to be applied to assist developing countries‘ economic development. If we think of stability as a situation in which the main macro variables are at a desired or target level.

In first part , I shall explain whether macro or micro economic method is more easily to predict or measure when and how and why the developing country's consumer shopping desire to be rised or reduced. Can we apply macroeconomic behavioral methods to help developing countries to control current rate of inflation, output or productive rising levels. It is necessary for the developing countries' economy to adjust from its current situation of instability to the target stabilised position.

In fact, any developing countries‘ economic in instability problem is reflecting in high inflation, low output growth and a growing balance of payment deficit. I shall indicate reasons whether we can apply macroeconomic behavioral methods to help developing countries to measure why and how and when consumer behavior or desire to be rised or reduced.

This book second part researches whether macro economic can measure how social change to influence positive or negative factor will impact any countries' crime rate to be raised or reduced. Has it relationship between global macro cconomic cnvironmcnt and young unemployed people whose behaviors change, e.g. attempting stealing when they encounter long term unemployment suitation or attempting to sell illegal drug to earn income or performing anit-social damage behavior to influence convenient road transportation and working people need catch amy public transportation tools etc. traffic jam manual causing anti-social damage behavior? Is poor macro economic environment main factor to influence crime number increases ?

Readers can make more accurate analysis to judge whether macro or micro economic methods can measure when and how and why social crime behaviors occurs as well as social consumer consumption desire why is rasied or reduced easily after you read this book.

Prologue

Table of content

Economic methods measure Consumer shopping desire changes

CHAPTER ONE

The national income measurement behavioral economy method

The national income accounting measurement is one good method to help any development countries to research whether what issues are their weaknesses or strengths is order to improve their economic development challenge. The central concept in national accouting is to measure the total output of products or services of the country's economy over a given time period.

The measure is known or gross domestic product (GDP). Output is produced by employing various factors of production (mainly labor and captial), and the revenue from sale of output of used to make payments to these factors of production. The value of output is identified, to the value of income paidout, or what is known as national income. Since the output produced is sold (or added to stocks), the value of output is also equal to the value of expenditure.

Hence, GDP can bre regarded as the value of output produced (appregate supply), the total value of expenditure on output (aggregate demand) or the total value of income in producing the output (real income). So, any developing countries can find whether how much or amout different industries value of output produced from and the real aggregate demand from consumers for different industries' products sale number or services demand in order find whether what factors cause the kind of industry's total GDP product sale number and real income reduction amount. For example, last year, the developing country's cloth industry sale number has 600,000 pieces and real GDP income has US$5 million. But, this year, its cloth industry sale number has 400,000 pieces and real GDP income has US$ 2 million. Hence, the developing countries can know its current year overall cloth industry sale number and GDP real income must reduce. Then, this country can attempt to find any factors had influenced itself cloth industry why this country itself cloth buyers number and their wearing demand has reduced. the reasons may include overall cloths price is exceed the normal price level or too high to compare its other foreign cloth sellers (overall local cloths price is exceed foreign cloth sellers' price extremely, or overall cloth fashion is not update or not attractive or quality is poor, or import cloth material producing price is too high to cause overall cloth sellers' cloth sale prices are needed to rise in order to earn balance profit or avoid reducing profit, or this developing country's cloth sellers' loyalties or brands are not famous to influence overall local cloth buyers know to choose to buy in itself country. Hence, this developing country can attempt to apply macroeconomic behavioral method to find whether what it/are the main factor(s) to cause its overall cloth industry's real GDP income and sale number is influenced to fall down suddenly in this year.

This macroeconomic country income measurement method can also measure why or what factors cause its any industries' overall supply and demand imbalance problem existence or cause. The reader will notice that the aggregate supply curve (AS) is drawn with an upward slope from left or right. So that at higher price levels more output is provided obviously, there will be a point when, given fixed amount of captial, labor and technology, output can not be increased in the short term.

This represents the full employment level, and at this point, the aggregrate suply curve will become vertical. The aggregate demand cuve simply shows the relationship between the total amount of products and services consumers desire and the price level. For one developing country's overall computer industry example, if it had overall aggregate supply of computer manufacturing number is one million pieces last year, but this year, it's aggregate supply of computer supply of computer manufacturing number is only five hundred thousand pieces. Hence, its overall computer aggregate manufacturing number fell down half pieces in this year.

But if it's overall computer buyers aggregate demand number climbed up from last year one million number to two million number this year. It means that this developing country has overall computer manufacturing number shortage problem to amy local computer sellers in this year. Why does it encounter computer manufacturing number shortage problem? The reasons may include: lacking high technological material supplies to manufacture any laptops or desktops for itself country's computer manufacturers, lacking technician labors to manufacture computers , it is possible due to many technicians choose to go to overseas to seek new computer manufacturing jobs, because they feel salaries are low or poor welfare from local computer employers, or computer manufacturers number decreases or close their businesses number increase, dismissing many computer technician labors , they are replaced by artifical intelligence or manufacturing machines, which are used to manufacture any computer products, or the country's overall computer manufacturing technology is not advanced to adapt to manufacture nowadays computer products.

On conclusion, any developing countries can apply national income measurement method to attempt to find what factor(s) cause(S) its aggregate supply and demand imbalance problem existence. Hence, national income measurement method is one kind of good macroeconomic behavioral method to measure or find why what reasons cause its some industries' products supply and demand number is imbalance or sale number and real GDP income decreases suddenly. Hence, any developing countries can apply macroeconomic analysis to find any factors to cause their any industries' development challenges in possible.

CHAPTER TWO

Industries economic methods

Industries economic theory explains how share the common feature of objectives for the firms (whether profit maximisation, growth of sales maximisation, satisfying etc.) and investigate the consequences of the pursuit of these objectives. Hence, industries economic theory can be attempted to find why the firm's customer number reduces, profir level is felt sudden higher to consumers, why customer's satisfactory level is low to the company's products. Due to the conduct of any firms covers the objectives, price-setting behavior, and attitudes to rivals (actual and potential). For example, if the country's publishing industry's competition rivals are more, due to it permits many overseas publishers enter to itseld domestic publishing market. So, its local publishers will feel more pressure to attract its readers to choose its local any publishers‘ books to buy because they have different countries' publishers choices to buy any books in their country.

Hence, the country's local publishing industry structural features of perfect different countries; publishers‘ competitions are a large number of overseas publishing firms of roughly equal size with free entry into this country's publishing industry suddenly. Even, this country's publishing industry book sellers does not plan to reduce their books sales prices or their books sale prices are not higher to compare their any one overseas publishers' books sale prices.

I believe that this country's local publishing firms readers number can not increase easy immediately because it is not the main reason of this country's overall local publishers‘ books sale prices are higher issue. It is due to its government permits many differen overseas countries' publishers free enter to itself local publishing market raise itself county's overall books sale effort for its local publoshers. So, it is unfaire to this country's local all publishers as well as free entry publishing market structure influences its all publishers' sale performance to improve easily. It ensures that a free entry market structure challenge to cause this country's publishers feel book sale difficult challenge.

The another case is that when many firms are grouped together as an industry and as firms which seell in the same market, e.g. perfect competition, homogenous, oligopoly and monopoly. In these causes, an industry's defined in terms of a product and the products of that product are members of the industry. Market and industry are very closely related in the case of homogenous products. It is assumed that each firm produces only one of a particular form to a specific industry in terms. If the nature of the firm's output and product which defined the industry.

What happens when a world of differentiated products and of multiproduct firms is considered? the existence of differentiated products can avoid these products which are close substitutes in demand. More formaly, a group of products (or services) is considered as close substitutes for each other when the cross or services is greater than some others. For example, if the country's computer industry has many similar laptop or desktop computer products are selling in itself country. When each groupinf the country's any computer brands products are close substitutes, but between any two kinds either desktop or laptop computer products in different computer brands grouping , the degree of substitution is low.

In this approach, the country's computer industry is defined in terms of high demand conditions to any brands of commputer firms in this country and it would be expected that the size of this country's computer industry would depend on the degree of substitutability used. Hence, it implies this country;s computer industry is very suitable to produce a homegencous computer product under similar or identical cost conditions, due to itself country's computer buyers won't easy to change their computer purchase choices, when they feel another brand computer firm (later another brand computer product choice) which can provide the similar computer brand product feature or function to replace their the early or prior computer brand product choice easily.

CHAPTER THREE

Applied more economic method solves consumer behavioral challenge

Can apply macro economic method to predict consumer variable behavior to any country? For example, when and how and why do the country consumers , they reduce shopping times or consumption desires in the country. For production and the labor market concept, production is integrated into the general equilibrium framework by firms. Firms utilize capital and labor to produce output and maximize the wealth of the agents who own them.

Households (house consumers) now maximize their utility through the consumption of commodities and leisure in themselves country. Households provide labor inputs to firms in return for wages in order to be able to obtain commodities. There are now markets for factor of production , capital and labor, in addition to commodity market.

In short run, the marginal product of labor (the extra amount of output obtained by adding another unit of labor) fulls as a firm takes on more employees. Profit-maximizing firms will increase employment to the level at which the revenue resulting from employment an additional employee equals the marginal cost of an extra employee. Thus, the lower the real wage, the higher the demand for labor. Individual workers maximize utility by choosing the optimium combinations of work and leisure and the supply of labor's defined as the level of employment forthcoming at a given real wage rate.

Hence, all who desire to find employment at the existing level of real wages will do so , when the country's employment condition and product sale number both are in equilibrium , due to the country's businessmen must have enough buyers number as well as their demands are still increasing. Then , the country's employers will choose to increase employees number or increase wage to attract them to help their businesses to increase more productivities.

So, it explains when on developing country has high unemployment ratio to compare other general developing countries . It implies that itself country's consumers' shopping desires will reduce or their shopping times will reduce, because their shopping desires reduce,, it influences the country's businessmens' products sale number will also reduce. Then, they will choose to reduce employees number or reduce their wages to compensate their sale loss in possible.

On conclusion, in macro economic view, it proves that it has direct or indirect case and effect relationship between the country itself employment rate and the year consumers overall shopping times or consumption desires level and overall market GDP (consumer expenditure overall amount in the year. It can apply the year employment rate number to measure whether the country's consumer shopping desires had been reducing or had been raising in the country in possible. Hence, any country's difference between the year employment ratio and last yeaar employment ratio which can explain why it's the year overall consumption market GDP amount had risen up or has fallen down in possible in order to predict what reasons cause this country's consumer shopping desires to be increase or decrease.

Chapter Four
Behavioral economy consumption desircs measurement method

How to apply behavioral economic theory to measure consumption level or consumption desire to the country? I shall assume that consumption is to be measured by private and public expenditures at constant prices at conventionally defined and all money prices are assumed constant. How to measure real consumption?

In fact, consumer behavior has relationship to any country, itself economic growth or recesion in any economic and consumption environment . The purpose of income calculations in practiced affairs to give consumers an indication of the amount which they can consume. It would seem that we ought to define a man's income as the maximum value, which he can consume during a week, and still expect to be well at the end of week as he has at the beginning.

An economy which uses money , but uses it is as a neutral link between transactions in real things and real assets and does not want of a better , a real exchange economy with an economy in which money plays a part of its own and affects motives and decisions and as , in short, one of the operative factors in the situation. So that the course of events can not be predicted either in the long period or in the short period, without knowledge of the behavior of money between the first state and last. It is a monetary economy means to influence any country itself consumer behavioral consumption desires change to more or less shopping times.

Hence, money matters in both the long and short run. Money affects real decision making and employment and output outcomes to any countries. The economic system is moving through calendar time from an irrevocable past to an uncertain and statistically unpredictable future.

Any country's past and present consumption market data do not necessary provide correct signals regarding future outcomes. Ths means that economic data are not necessarily generated by a process. Constrasts denominated in money terms are a human in an entrepreneurial economy. It helps humans efficiently organize time-consuming production and exchange processes in a world of uncertainty.

In any money using entreprensurial economy, entrepreneurs‘ decisions regarding production and hiring depend on expectations of receiving contractual sales revenues (cash inflows) in excess of the contractual money costs of production (cash outflows). Since, the money wage contract is the most efficient oriented contracts, modern economies can be characterized as money-wage contract-based systems.

Hence, money processes two essential elasticity that differentiate is from the products of industry. These describe why (a) money does not grow on trees (money's elasticity of production is zero)and (b) why producible products are not good liquid stores of value (the elasticity of substitution between liquid assets , such as money and producible products is zero).

If money has these elasticity , then unemployment develops, that is to say, because people can not be employed, when the object of desire (i.e. money, good useful product or good quality product , even shopping enjoyable feeling,) is something which can not produced and the demand of shopping desires are reduced to the country's people.

Hence, unemployment rather than full employment is a normal outcome in any entrepreneurial, market oriented, money-contract-using system in a free competition market environment to the country. So, when the country's people consumption desires are reduced in possible , because unemployment rare rises or living of cost rises, general products prices rise, a spot or commodity price inflation etc. different factors. Then, they will influence the country's economic recession occurrence more easily.

Thus, any countries leaders can not neglect the relationship between unemployment and consumption desire and economic growth or recession relationship. Because in long term, unemployment ratio rises, it has possible to bring many consumers their shopping desires to be reduced as well as economic recession effect to the country.

It implies that any countries' consumers desires, which has relationship to whether themselves jobs supplying number is enough to let themselves countries' people to work. However, labor shortage issue must be better to compare job supplying shortage issue to any country, because labor shortage won't influence consumers' shopping desires to be reduced absolute. It will influence any businesses' productivities are less or reaching the low productive level. Otherwise, jobs supplying shortage will influence consumers' shopping desires to be reduced in the country. It is possible due to the country has many people lose their jobs suddenly. Then, they can not accept to spend money to buy too much any things in their countries easily.

On conclusion, any countries' consumer behaviors or consumption desires must have relationship to themselves countries' jobs supplying number. Hence, any countries leaders need to concern whether themselves countries have enough jobs supply to let low education or high education people to work in order to satisfy their living needs in nowadays societies.

CHAPTER FOUR

Behavioral economy consumption desires measurement method

How to apply behavioral economic theory to measure consumption level or consumption desire to the country? I shall assume that consumption is to be measured by private and public expenditures at constant prices at conventionally defined and all money prices are assumed constant. How to measure real consumption?

In fact, consumer behavior has relationship to any country, itself economic growth or recesion in any economic and consumption environment . The purpose of income calculations in practiced affairs to give consumers an indication of the amount which they can consume. It would seem that we ought to define a man's income as the maximum value, which he can consume during a week, and still expect to be well at the end of week as he has at the beginning.

An economy which uses money , but uses it is as a neutral link between transactions in real things and real assets and does not want of a better , a real exchange economy with an economy in which money plays a part of its own and affects motives and decisions and as , in short, one of the operative factors in the situation. So that the course of events can not be predicted either in the long period or in the short period, without knowledge of the behavior of money between the first state and last. It is a monetary economy means to influence any country itself consumer behavioral consumption desires change to more or less shopping times.

Hence, money matters in both the long and short run. Money affects real decision making and employment and output outcomes to any countries. The economic system is moving through calendar time from an irrevocable past to an uncertain and statistically unpredictable future.

Any country's past and present consumption market data do not necessary provide correct signals regarding future outcomes. Ths means that economic data are not necessarily generated by a process. Constrasts denominated in money terms are a human in an entrepreneurial economy. It helps humans efficiently organize time-consuming production and exchange processes in a world of uncertainty.

In any money using entreprensurial economy, entrepreneurs‘ decisions regarding production and hiring depend on expectations of receiving contractual sales revenues (cash inflows) in excess of the contractual money costs of production (cash outflows). Since, the money wage contract is the most efficient oriented contracts, modern economies can be characterized as money-wage contract-based systems.

Hence, money processes two essential elasticity that differentiate is from the products of industry. These describe why (a) money does not grow on trees (money's elasticity of production is zero)and (b) why producible products are not good liquid stores of value (the elasticity of substitution between liquid assets , such as money and producible products is zero).

If money has these elasticity , then unemployment develops, that is to say, because people can not be employed, when the object of desire (i.e. money, good useful product or good quality product , even shopping enjoyable feeling,) is something which can not produced and the demand of shopping desires are reduced to the country's people.

Hence, unemployment rather than full employment is a normal outcome in any entrepreneurial, market oriented, money-contract-using system in a free competition market environment to the country. So, when the country's people consumption desires are reduced in possible , because unemployment rare rises or living of cost rises, general products prices rise, a spot or commodity price inflation etc. different factors. Then, they will influence the country's economic recession occurrence more easily.

Thus, any countries leaders can not neglect the relationship between unemployment and consumption desire and economic growth or recession relationship. Because in long term, unemployment ratio rises, it has possible to bring many consumers their shopping desires to be reduced as well as economic recession effect to the country.

It implies that any countries' consumers desires, which has relationship to whether themselves jobs supplying number is enough to let themselves countries‘ people to work. However, labor shortage issue must be better to compare job supplying shortage issue to any country, because labor shortage won't influence consumers' shopping desires to be reduced absolute. It will influence any businesses' productivities are less or reaching the low productive level. Otherwise, jobs supplying shortage will influence consumers' shopping desires to be reduced in the country. It is possible due to the country has many people lose their jobs suddenly. Then, they can not accept to spend money to buy too much any things in their countries easily. On conclusion, any countries' consumer behaviors or consumption desires must have relationship to themselves countries' jobs supplying number. Hence, any countries leaders need to concern whether themselves countries have enough jobs supply to let low education or high education people to work in order to satisfy their living needs in nowadays societies.

CHAPTER FIVE

International war economy influences consumer behavior

1.1 Can wars impact global economy threat?

1.1.1 How did First World War influence Europe economy ?

Can wars bring either advantages or disadvantages or both to impact our economy growth ?In history, I feel that international war can influence any country's economy development has either positive or negative impact in possible.

On the inflationary hand, for the First World War economy growth influence example, in the First World War and since most notably the German hyperinflation of the 1920 year, this type of monetary regime shows a far smaller tendency towards inflation. In the First World War period, volatility of inflation and output were higher in the short run. So, First World War had little negative impact to influence world inflation in the war period. However, in the First World War period, the supply of money was determined not by the rates of economic growth only, but by the amount of available gold and could not be adjusted in response to economic needs. So, new sources of gold would increase money supply and inflation and decrease interest rates , the opposite of what modern central banks would do to provide stable economic growth in First World War. So, it explained that the First World War occurrence caused the change from non-inflationary to inflationary long term development. Thus, it seems First World War brings more money supply and gold supply to stable economic growth in the future long term period.

On the labor productivity influence hand, leaving monetary issues aside, the First World War created the working time intellectual mood to change labor productivity, it would be a 15-18 hours working week for more enlightened leisure to Europe labors. Some prominent modern economists on the accuracy of the predictions on GDP growth per capital was remarkably accurate given to be fallen down that it was made at the time when economy growth theory did not even exist in the First World War period. Thus, it seems First World War also causes working time to be raised to the developing countries during the industrialization period. Then, the long time working time brought to the developing countries‘ workers to it is poor for labor health. Hence, although employers can raise productivity, but they need many workers to work long time to cause unhealthy. The majority found that the prediction on leisure is of the variations between world regions , due to income level exist, making European variety of capitalism. So, the First World War caused income inequality within countries and between nation states, trends in working hours , world poverty and ever growing needs (consumerism) and the like. Thus, the developed western countries' workers can work lesser time to compare to the developing Asia countries‘ workers. Consequently, First World War brought negative impact to influence the developing Asia countries' worker unhealthy and physical and mental illnesses number had been increasing as well as it brought positive impact to influence the labor productivity had been increasing to the Asia countries‘ employers, due to their workers need to work long time every day.

It seems on the positive impact hand, that the First World War caused the inflation occurrence to bring more money supply and gold supply to be raised to influence global economic growth. But, on the negative impact hand, it also brought low working hours in European developed countries and high working hours to the Asia developing countries which are needed to do different occupations in developing countries as well as the income inequality caused unfair social challenge had also occurred in developed countries, such as Europe, UK, US etc. and developing countries, such as China, Japan, Korea etc . Thus, First World War had brought developed countries better economy development and better salary and less working hours to labors because Europe had reached the mature stage of industrialization to avoid labors who needed to work overtime. Otherwise, it had brought developing countries poor economy development and poor salary and labors need work long time to raise productivities.

In conclusion, it implied that the First World War had bought some bad influences to developing countries' economic system, e.g. social income inequality, working hours inequality, inflation and GDP per capita going down in the past Europe economic history development, but it also bought welfares to developed countries' European labor working time intellectual mood to change labor productivity, it would be a 15-18 hours working week for more enlightened leisure to Europe labors. So, it seemed to cause negative economic influence to developing countries, but it cause positive economic influence to developed counties during the First World War time.

● Are US poor economic consequences of war?

What are the macroeconomic effects of US government spending on the war? I believe modern times are that the human cost military spending has created positive economic outcomes for the US economy. I shall indicate how the human costs of war influences positive economic outcomes for the US on these aspects which include: GDP, consumption , investment , inflation and income distribution aspects.

In fact, US heightened military spending can create employment additional economic activity and contributes to the military weapon development of new technologies, which can bring advantages into other industries in US. For long term economic influence, US military weapon research and development on creating employment would potentially have the same low cost economic benefit in US. For example, US economy had higher GDP growth in the Afghanistan and Iraq war period. Another benefit is that US had appropriate conditions for future growth after the Second World War great depression period. It was a sharp decline in income inequality and the trend in declining inequality standard after the Second World War great depression period. Thus, America's human cost military spending could bring indirect military weapon research and development on creating employment benefit and it would potentially have the same low cost economic benefit in US. However, in the war period, the higher levels of government military weapon spending with war tends to generate some positive economic benefits in the short-term period, specifically through increases in economic growth during spending booms after war period.

Why it can bring GDP growth in the US war period. In general, by the end of World Ward II, US GDP was over 120 % and tax revenue increased more than three times to over 20% of GDP. However, GDP growth there was are increase in the trend lines after the war had finished when unemployment was eliminated, recovery was well underway prior to the war, are the key counterfactual is whether similar spending on US public works would have generated even more growth. However, US macroeconomic history over the past seventy years, that there are a number of negative economic effects from conducting any wars. But, there have also positive benefits of increases US government spending on military industry. Moreover, when an economy has excess capacity and unemployment , it is possible that increasing military spending can provide an important stimulus. When military and defense spending is important in providing security for the US nation as well as helping to support and protect US's national affect.

So, in war economic view point, it will bring this question: Is efficiency or justification for any particular macroeconomic effects of war spending for US? To answer this question, I shall suppose security is not only dependent on an adequate military capability , but security can also keep on economic stability. For example, price controls strategy and rationing strategy had a significant role to play to influence consumption in US, during war period. For example, it was difficult for household to purchase products , such as washing machines, irons or water heaters because the raw resources, e.g. steel and production capabilities are needed to be used to produce military weapons instead of these products effort to prepare to fight the enemy in the Second World War. So, the raw resources, e.g. steel price will be rasied, due to shortage to supply to produce the home consumer products , Then, it will bring the home consumer products price to be raised. So, war will bring negative impact to influence home consumer product prices to be raised, due to shortage of steel resources supply when they are supplied to produce weapon to win enemy in war period. Consequently, In war period negative resource shortge hand, as the same time, the war production board was able to assign priorities to scare materials, such as rubber, steel and aluminum to ensure which went to production of the military, rather than to civilian products. In addition, wages were controlled and personal savings were encouraged through the purchase of war bonds which further limited the size of individual's disposable income during the Second World War period.

Moreover, in the war period, it also bring food price raising, due to food supply shortage and poor living standrd to poor people, even rich people. Due to people were also encouraged to conserve food and produce as much of that own food as possible because food items were generally scare. Freezes were also stayed for wages. Combined with a general reduction in consumption, it can be said living standards for whose already employed, at least in material terms did not improved , even to rich people. It means that war will influence people quality of life to be fallen down.

Even, in terms of total GDP. Such as World War II (WWII) did not create a permanent increase or change in the growth the trend after the war had ended. However, the positive lasting effort for WWII was a more even distribution of wealth. This reallocation of income created the ideal conditions for the formation of an advancement consumer economy till to nowadays.

However, on war long time influence hand, the WWII influenced US economy to be changed to be better, such as material well being was affected by tax increases, new price and wage controls which constrained private sector consumption and investment is encouraged, due to World War II had destroyed the traditional material development, so it also encouraged new investors to invest to any Asia or Europea new businesses.

- Can war economy policy influence peace and security?

I believe war economics policy may contribute to international peace and security as positive impact more than negative impact. The reasons are as below:

A first positive attitude behavioral possibility , any war economic policy can increase international interdependence through trade and finance raises the potential costs of war to a degree that makes welfare an irrational option of foreign policy can raise economic growth and builds good trading relationship between countries. Moreover, the use of superior economic and military power to harm an actual or potential aggressor's economy and make it stops preparing of waging war, e.g. US restricted Mexico imported to itself country, US invented military weapons to threaten to Korea to avoid nuclear war occurrence. In the past, US spent to military expenditure which could rise to employ soldier numbers to reduce unemployment as well as assisted military weapon manufacturers needed to employ many manufacturing workers to manufacture many military weapons for US government military fighting need.

Hence, the relationship between war and economy will bring this basic question: Whether either can economics provide a growing tool for avoiding war or whether may consumption for resources and markets result in an increased likelihood of war? Following the increase of international trade and financial transfers in modern times. However, there has been a growing to concern the economic wisdom of war.

Liberal economists oppose the idea that war might be a good business and advocated the promotion of peace and advocated the promotion of peace by international economic links among the different countries. Although, history has shown that enlightened economic self-interest was not always alike to contribute to the ultimate avoidance of war. But, a short overview of the liberal peace theory indicates, it takes a look at the amount ability of economic instruments as a means to enforce peace by an economically superior country or group of countries, e.g. within the framework of the United Nations or of regional organization for security and cooperation in Europe, the African Union or the organization of American States.

1.1.4 How civil wars influence positive or negative impact?

On country itself civil war negative impact hand, what is the impact of civil wars on economic growth at domestic and in nearby countries? Some economists believe civil war can have a profound negative influence on the economic fortunes of a country or its neighbors, e.g. owing to a loss of human capital, a destruction of infrastructure and reductions in investment and trade and daily market activities. Within the period of measurement have economic consequences , the economists scale the civil war variable to be better identify their relative impacts. They indicate the distance between countries which is a factor provides the most accurate measure of the negative economic consequences of civil wars on other countries.

On country itself civil war positive impact hand, in economic view point, the country itself civil war indicates the income and capital input terms. Since, everything is in per capita terms. Due to civil war encourage technological development. Technology changes are in the investment in labor effectiveness. The capital includes physical and human capital . How civil war influences efficiency growth . The growth in labor's enhanced efficiency is from technology change and capital depreciation. So, anything that can raise labor growth or its improved efficiency, increases the denominator or capital per capita and so reduced its growth and that of incomer per capita. Depreciation or the gradual wearing down of capita; through use or age also limits capital growth. Some economists suggest that war migration is a good growth of labor to influence the immigration country's economic growth. For example, the inflow of refugees from a nearby civil war can lead to in-migration and adversely affect income per capita growth. Migration may , however, influences the in-migration country economic growth if the migrants bring in human capital, due to civil war.

Consequently, from a theoretical perspective, civil wars can adversely affect income per capita growth at home through a number of avenues. So civil war will cause bad influence to home country, the reasons are as below:

The reasons include:

First, a civil conflict can destroy physical and human capital. Second, by the international trade flows, and day-to-day marketing activities, civil wars can inhibit growth. Third, civil wars may divert the inflow of foreign direct investment (FDI) owing to heightened perceived risks of investors. Because (FDI) perceived is an imported source of savings that finances investment. So, a fill in FDI results in reduced growth. Heightened instability and risks will also limit investment at home and cause a flight of savings abroad. Fourth, civil wars cause indirect government defense expenditures from productive social overhead capital e.g. roads, public schools and bridges, gardens to less productive defense spending. Fifth, such wars may cause the internal displacement of people as their homes either come under serious control or are destroyed. So that income per capita is adversely influenced. Sixth, civil wars often result in the breakdown of the health lead to lack of medical care, less clean drinking water and reduced sanitation , all of which have negative consequences on economic activities and growth .

Thus, any country itelf civil war can bring negative impacts more than positive impacts. Due to economic impacts may even increase further from some conflicts as nearby countries reduce trade with others in the regions and potential investors brand , even non-neighboring countries have as poor investment risks. Thus, there are four potential channels , such as human capital, physical capital, labor growth and an intercept shift are influenced by civil wars as well as which can influence income per capita growth in other nearby countries. To conclude, neighboring countries need to concern how to avoid civil war is caused to occur among themselves because civil wars will have negative impact to influence their economic growth.

● How economic positive and negative impact of the war to higher military spending?

Most models show that military spending to divert resources from productive uses, such as consumption and investment , and ultimately slows economic growth and reduces employment. So, it seems war causes disadvantages more than advantages to influence economy growth to any countries in possible.

Some economists showed global insight produced a set of projections that compared a scenario with an increase in annual military spending equal to 1.0% of GDP current about $135billions relative to its baseline scenario . This is approximately equal to the increase in defense spending that has taken place compared with the pre-Sept. 11th terrorism Iraq war baseline to US government higher military spending. However, who also indicated military spending is not generally perceived to cost jobs.

In standard economic models, war its positive impact can be thought of in the same way as spending on the environment from war bad influence. When tax and emission restrictions are often used to achieve environment protection during and after war. It is also possible to reach environmental targets by paying people to do things that will reduce pollution. For example, it is possible to reduce greenhouse gas emissions by paying people to buy more fuel efficient cars and appliances, or paying than to install insulation and other energy saving devices. So, during the war period, more greenhouse gas fuel efficient cars will increase demand in car market. Thus, war can reduce air and water pollution cost and encourage greenhouse gas fuel consumption. In the case of both increased military spending and paying people to take steps to reduce greenhouse gas emissions, resources would be reduced to supply to these countries' domestic market directed uses.

In standard economic models, war it's negative impact to this redirection of other resources, due to the original resources are used to increase military spending to manufacturing any new weapons and it will cause this original resources are shortage to prepare for these countries' manufacturing countries. So, these resources shortage challenges will cause these military spending countries' economy to operate less efficiently and therefore lead to slower growth and fewer jobs supplies. Thus, war will bring resource shortage challenges and fewer jobs supplies bad influence. In policy debates, it is important to recognize the potential jobs losses are caused from military spending factor mainly. Also the potential economic costs are often a factor in debates over environment policy.

Due to war causes the military countries' air and water pollution challenges. So, the military countries' wars occurrence will raise the water and air pollution cost of chance. It is often believed environmental pollution challenge has relationship between wars and increases in military spending. So, in this way, any country is carrying on military spending is comparable in most models to any other form of any country's spending, such as spending on public products or improving the environment pollution expenditures. Thus, it seems war will bring environment pollution economic cost more than environment protection economic benefit to any military expending countries.

Country internal civil war influences consumer behavior

2.1 The relationship between country itself internal civil war and human welfare

2.1.1 How internal civil war influences human welfare?

Nowadays, a growing number of economists and political scientists often ask this simple question: Why there is so much civil wars in any country itself the world? Poverty is commonly held to be a leading cause of internal wars. Indeed, it has close relationship between low per capita incomes and higher propensities for internal war's countries. Such as developing country Africa, it has many times more internal wars. So, it brings poverty and low living standards and poor health and poor air and water pollution environment to let African to live. Then, hunger and disease will also be caused easily in Africa.

However, internal civil wars also bring negative influences to developed countries, such as Australia, US Canada, UK , Japan, Korea etc. countries. The reason is because the internal civil war counties which refugee flows will choose to immigrate to those developed countries. Such as developing countries, South Korea and Africa and India , there have many times more internal civil wars .So it brings poverty and low living standards and poor health and poor environment to let African , South Korean, Indian to choose to live to these developed countries. Then, hunger and disease will be caused easily in developing and developed both countries, due to developed countries permit these developing countries' refugee who immigrate to themselves countries to live from internal civil war counties refugee immigration easily.

Moreover, internal civil war can also influence developed countries, such as Australia, US, Canada , UK refugee flows will choose to immigrate to these developed countries lawlessness as well as the illicit trades in drugs , arms and minerals will appear into these developed countries neighboring conflict zones . The destructive consequences of internal civil welfare may be a great as to potentially be a factor in the growing gap between the world's richest and poorest nations.

2.1.2 Can internal civil wars influence the country's long run economic development?

Has it relationship between long run economic growth and internal civil war? Some economists recommend that it focuses on impacts on capital and population, the basic of economic production and whether the internal civil war country is possible rapid recovery as well as the internal civil wars cause economic impacts which can also been found for human capital, including measures of education, nutrition, health and productivity to the internal civil war countries.

What are intenal civil war negative impacts? Some behavior economists had experimented one interesting research to indicate that any internal civil war country will reduce human resource productivity growth , will reduce overall GDP in possible. Their research indicated the internal war armed group leaders are most motivate citizens to be soldiers for their side. Participation becomes easier to motivate the lower is citizen's opportunity cost of fighting . So there models predict that the amount of citizens' time devoted to fighting increases as the returns to fighting rise relative to the returns to reduce human resources supply to society to assist enterprises to raise any productive activities.

Consequently, in economic view point, if the internal civil war countries citizen will be trained to be soldiers. Then, it will reduce citizen to do other occupations in the internal war period. Also, the internal civil war countries will reduce their citizen have time and effort to do other social occupations to assist countries' economy development in the internal civil war period. Moreover, the internal civil war countries citizen, such as human resource number will be shortage to supply to satisfy their countries' enterprises' needs in the internal civil war period. It will influence economic growth to be go down during the internal civil war period to the internal civil war countries for either short term or long term. Even, the natural resource supply, e.g. water, food, vehicle gas etc. will be concentrate on spending to satisfy the soldiers' needs. It will cause natural resource shortage to supply to satisfy to citizen's life needs daily in the natural civil war period. So, the internal civil war will bring disadvantage to influence economic growth to the internal civil war countries.

2.1.3 How can reduce the risks of the civil internal war to influence economy growth?

How can reduce the risks when internal civil war occurs in the country? What factors explain variations in the duration of civil internal wars, and why should policymakers care? I shall suppose to the duration of civil internal wars , which should be implicated in their destructiveness to the civil internal war country as well as long time duration of civil internal wars should have long time poor economic influence to the civil internal war country.

At any given point in a civil internal war, the civil internal war country government (A) and the civil internal war country rebels(B) each must choose between stopping or continuing to flight.

This implies four possible outcomes from their joint decisions at any time.

The first outcome is that if (B) continues flight and (A) stops, (B) wins and the government (A) is overthrown.

The second outcome is that if government (A) flights and (B) stops, (A) wins and the revolt is defeated (B) .

The third outcome is that if both (A) and (B) choose to stop flight at the same time, the civil internal war ends to be a negotiated settlement.

The fourth outcome is that if neither decides to stop, the civil internal war continues (Stam 1996 , 34-37).

Stam (1996, 353) again indicated the four outcomes can be represented as an two person game. Continued flight is the dominant strategy for both sides.

Thus, it seems negotiated settlement is the best solution to solve any civil internal war because it won't have either win or loss outcome to either of party, it will have win outcome to both countries.

In economic welfare view point, they will discuss how to earn the much economic benefits to achieve the reasonable negotiation fairly. It is a two parties win-to-win method to both supported government and not supported government parties both. Because usually the cause of any internal civil war , due to the not supported (disagreed) government party feel whose government is unfair to give reasonable and fair much economic welfare to them in society. So, they (part of citizen) only choose to cause internal civil war to let their country to know that who feel dissatisfactory at the time.

In economic view point, unfair resource allocation challenge will cause any internal civil war easily in any country. Thus, it means that any country government ought to know when and how to allocate its limited resources to let its citizen to feel fair to use (spend) in society when resources are not shortage to supply to them to consume. Also, it means how to allocate (spend) limited resource to prepare any countries' citizen to enjoy to consume. So, it is one important question to any country government to concern if which wanted to reduce internal civil war occurrence chance on nowadays societies. Thus, it seems that any country itself internal civil war will bring disadvantages more than advantages.

Bibliography

Stam , A. C. 1996, Win, Lose or Draw: Domestic politics and the crucible of war . Ann Arbor: University of Michigan Press.

CHAPTER SIX

Macro economic-inflation consumption and the savings ratio consumer desire measurement

Any countries have chance to encounter inflation problem. Inflation means as a factor that could reduce the saving ration. If consumers expected prices to rise, they would bring forward consumption to take advantage of lower prices. For example, during the 1970s , as both inflation and the saving ration rose theories were advanced to explain why inflation could lead to an increase in saving.

The most clear or reasonable explanation is that households do not base their consumption decisions about consumption and saving on their money income alone consumption and saving on their money income alone, due to they reduce some capital losses from their income. In particular, they reduce some reduction in the real value of monetary assets caused by inflation. So, inflation could affect the savings ratio, due to gains and losses on loans between households cancel out. It depends on where some households deposit money with banks.

How can consumption function explain it has relationship between the savings ratio and inflation have been suggested by some economists ? The reasons may include as below:

(1) There may be a link between changes in income and changes in consumption. If consumption during a quarter is related to money income in the previous quarter, then a acceleration (accumulation) in wages and

prices will lead to a fall in real consumption in the quarter following the accumulation, and in a rise in the savings ratio. So, it explains why money incomes and savings will have risen , but real consumption will long fallen. Because the inflation influences the incomes and savings seem rise, but in fact, if the consumption amouts and numbers do not rise when the inflation period. The country's consumers‘ whose shopping desires or real consumptions do not real rise as the same time in the period. Unless, the country's general consumers can accept to spend much expenditure to buy more number of any things in themselves societies. Otherwisem, the real consumption effect will not be achieved in the country.

(2) The uncertainty created by a high and unstable rate of inflation could cause people to save more. The degree of uncertainty is difficult to quantify and may not be tied to the inflation rate in a simple linear relationship. So, due to any countries' citizen or consumers or living people who must not predict when inflation will come. Because this uncertain when inflation occurrence reason, many consumers will not change their habit consumption behaviors, such as habitly spending much consumers, they won't change their consumption habits to be reduced number or consumption times easily or habitly spending less consumers, they won't change their consumption habits to be raised number or consumption times easily. Even, they predict inflation will come as soon. Because inflation predicting feeling will be more uncertain to influence their spending behaviors changing more easily. Unless the country's government can ensure to notice its citizen when inflation will come, then it will influence their shopping times or consumption number to be changed easily.

(3) The personal factor includes businesses, and stock or share investment appreciation during periods of inflation may boost savings. So, the county will have many citizen choose to save more money to bank if they feel inflation will come as soon in possible. They won't like to spend much expenditure to buy any things easily because they will feel unreasonable price or unfair purchase and sale transaction in social market in the moment.

(4) Unexpected inflation favours bank borrowers (bank debtors) and bank itself (bank creditors) both roles. So, it tends to favour the young who borrow to buy houses, or much entertainment consumption enjoyment spending when they feel inflation will occur to influence house price to be rised or any things and entertainment expenditures to be rised also. Because if banks informed inflation will be occur in possible soon, this

prediction will let the feeling long term living house needed buyers whom will choose to borrow much money in order to buy any houses in the short time. They aim to avoid inflation causes general houses price to be risen and bringing unreasonable and unfair house purchase prices when inflation is real occurred soon. Thus, the bank creditors marginal propensity to same could be lower that of debtors (bank borrowers).

I believe that it has close relationship between income saving ratio and inflation and consumption desire. Such as the economist keynes's (1981) hypothesis assumes that some degree supported by the proportion of income saved increased as income ought rise or the same live in general countries' consumption condition or economic environment. He indicated that , for example, there are other explanation for the rising British savings ratio during 1960 s. His opinions were based on below evidences:

(1) The low savings ratio cria 1950 s was a reaction to shortage of products and forced saving during war time and the early post war period. When many types of products were not variable to buy or were rationed. The rising savings ratio during the 1950 s probably contained an accurate prediction of recovery a normal level.

(2) There were demographic and social changes factors in UK in between 1950s and 1960s. The principle change was the spread of pension funds. This increased the level of committed saving as the proportion of the UK population who were members of pension schemes increased, though a part of saving through pension schemes may be offset by a reduction in other forms of saving, e.g. net saving through life insurance schemes increased from 5.7 % of PDI between 1960s and 1981 year.

So, changes in UK population structure in this period are another factor influencing the savings ratio. Children are expensive any may cause a fall in income as well, consumption function in the direction of increased saving. Any increase in the UK proportion of married women in the UK working population could have increased the saving ratio. On the other side, the increasing proportion of the UK elderly in the UK population probably reduce it. On conclusion, the influence saving ratio raising factors to the country UK which may include: raising the country's population beween 1960s to 1981s which may include: the children and elderly number increase or decrease, pension and insurance product saving plan, lacking enough variable kinds of products choice to let consumers buy after war period main factors and inflation main factors. So, it impact consumer shopping desire will fall down to UK in the after war period between 1960s.

and 1981s.

On conclusion, if the country hope to raise consumer desire, the methods may include that banks discourage saving interest reducing or stable staying plan and insurance plans promotion, inflation will come soon information, young population immigration number increases, creating many jobs to low and high education people to work, exciting employers raise salary, encouraging rent houses choice to house buyers. However, macro economic-inflation consumption and the savings ratio can be the best method to predict whether consumer desire will rise up or fall down to the country because if the country has many people have already saved money to bank, it implies that many people do not like to buy any things, due to they feel inflation will come soon. Otherwise, when if the country has less people decide to save money to bank, it implies that many people like to buy any things, due to they feel inflation will not come soon. So, it ought have close relationship between the saving ratio and inflation and consumption desire to any countries.

Source: Economic trends, Nov. 1981, p.16

CHAPTER SEVEN

Micro or macro economic method consumer desire measurement

The role of economy can measure consumer behavior, it can be used to analyze and gather social data, e.g. how many different brands of product are selling in the country, how many youth people, working people, old peole age groups are living in the country, how many the kind of product number is sold in the yar, how many average shopping times to the kind product to the country overall consumers number in the year, how long useful time to be replaced another new product , the counry's consumers they use the kind of product. Consequently, economist can conclude the effect of the kind of product sale number, different age of consumers' purchase times and useful time etc. different market data in order to predict whether the kind of product ought be manufactured how many number which is the most suitable number as well as whether the reasonable price level is to achieve the most highest sale income to the country's the kind of brand product next year.

In general, consumer behavioral research economists have improved the research task of analysing and predicting econmic change how it can influence consumer behavior. A great deal of econometic work has been devoted to building and testing models, that is systems of relationships designed to how the interdependent variation of a set of variable, and with estimating the constants in these consumer behavioral influence models.

Moreover, a system of equations in which the values of some variables appear for consecutive time periods can be used for any countries' consumer behavioral changing prediction purposes , but the predictions which can be dervied express the way in which the system would vary through time if it were allowed to run undistributed. Ths aspect ot the research consumer behavioral changing matter is now recognized and specifies the assumed properties , since they have importance bearing not only in prediction, but also on the estimation, e.g. how and why and when the country's consumer purchase habit will sudden change. Hence, the consumer behavioral research economists' role is to provide the country's market information about the systematic factors at work , so that the variable element of guess-work is reduced as far as possible.

All practical economists who are not econometricians will readily assent to this statement as it relates to identities or definitions. No one in his senses will be content with predictions: what the most minimum of income level influences consumer individual shopping desire reduces, what the most minimum of savings level influences general consumers' shopping desires reduce etc. which do not satisfy the usual accounting identifies.

Economics is the science which indicates human (consumer) role is as a relationship between (achieving sale effect) and consumers feel scarce to buy the product (psychological response), because general consumers feel scarce or shortage supplying to the product in themselves coutry market. They will choose to attempt to visit any shops to buy the product immediately. So, scarce or shortage supplying factor may be one important factor to influence general consumers expect to buy the kind of product immediately if they feel the brand of product is shortage to sell to them in any shops in the country. It may be more important to compare cheaper price factor, inflation factor, the shop's geographical location far away to the consumer individual home factor, savings or investment etc. different factors to influence the country's consumers purchase desires to be rised up or fallen down.

The economc methods measure consumer behaviors (purpose to accept primary facts. Hence is on the quantitative side a further type of information. By primary facts, I mean such things as the originating entries in a firm's sale cash book or the quantity of some commodity produced over a particular period. On the other hand, there are many items, similar to primary facts in the actual world, but which are not capable of being in the same simple manner, e.g. the income of an individual or a nation GDP. These data is the best consumer behavioral changing to the country's social consumption market.

The principle problems which the answering of questions of fact sets to the economic statisticans can conveniently be analyzed in the familiar terms of demand and supply concerns to research how, why and when the kind of product's consumer shopping desires whether they will like to choose either buy more or less to the kind of product. We first have to decide what we want to know and then consider how we are going to find it out.

For the point of view of the user of factual information. The obvious approach to the research how, why and when consumer shopping desires change to the kind of product purchase choice issue. A system for ascertaining facts which worked on this principle, such as how many economic facts are ascertained to the country's consumption market concerns to the kind of product. There is no point in trying to ascertain the national income on some given definition to the nearest pounds or UK dollar measured when in fact no use for the information could be concerned that required it to be accurate to more than the nearest 10 million pound or UK dollar for England, UK GDP (Gross Domestic Product) income in the year. Hence, GDP is not the most suitable data gathering method to be used to analyze why , how and when consumers behavioral change to the kind of product sale in the country. Because ir is one macro economic view, it is not more accurate to compare micro economic view to measure any country's consumer behavior or shopping desire changes , such as individual income level changes,. Otherwise, these micro economic data ,such as firms sale number and sale income changes etc. data they are more suitable to be used in order to measure whether the kind of product's consumption desire will increase or decrease more accurate for the country next year.

On economics, we meet with a number of different kinds of mathematical relationship. Perhaps the simplest is the definitional relationship which certains only variables linked together which certains only variables linked together by the arithmatic. Examples of such relationships are: Income equals consumption plus saving, the sim of saving by each sector of the economy equals the total saving of economy, the quantity of some commodity sold multiplied by average selling price equals the expenditure on the commodity. These equations do not tell use anything about the behavior of economic agents e.g. consumer behavior: they imply indicate the defined relationships between certain terms. When relationships of this kind form part of a system of equations. They may be used to eliminate certain variable from the system and thus reduce the degrees of freedom of the system.

To go back to the example of the definitional relationship " income equals consumption plus saving", we can obviously calculate it means that income minus consumption, whereever saving appears in a system of relationships. Thus, reducing the number of variables and of equation. As ny explanation indicates that why micro economic data, e.g. indivdual income variable level, saving variable level is more accuate to be gathered to use for judgement when, why and how the kind of product general consumers behaviors or shopping desires change to compare macro economic data , e.g. the country's GDP in the country. Because we can not build up a theory of human behavior with the aid of definitional relationship alone, in addition we shall need relationship of age groups, such as a individual or a young age group, working age group, old age group different age consumers or occupation groups, e.g. professional occupation, such as teacher, doctor, lawyer , or low educational level occupation, such as factory worker etc. different age or occupation consumer groups of a consumption behaviouristic or consumer group character telling us something of the way in which the different individuals or consumer groups behavr or indicating the technical relationships which subsist between, say the input of factors of production and the output of product. Example of such relationships are: The familiar demand and supply to the brand product relationships; the relationship connecting saving to the individual income or general young age group income or old age group income or working people income in the society, and the rate of interest to the country's bank system; a relationship indicating the presence or absence of price control to gas issue concerns how to influence car buyers' purchase cars demands or driving desires. All of these any one of micro economic relationship is the influence of as aspect of the consumer behavioral changing or consumer desire changing system highly relevant to general macro economic behavioral change system to the country.

Is these any advantage in operate with structural equations? The answer is " yes" for the following reasons. In the case of relationship expressing behavior these may be expected to ahve the highest possible degree of performance, since they reflect the behavior of only one type of entity in the system, such as sales and price information equations just mentioned, depend for their stability on the constant responses not of one but of two or more types of entity, in the example both buyers (the kind of product consumers or buyers) and sellers (the kind of product sellers). Thus, if we can assume that the buyers' responses , through not the sellers' responses will remain constant over a period, we can express (or forecast) the quantity transacted by using one equation if we adopt the demand equation. Whereas, we shall need to least two if we adopt that sales equation. Thus, in micro economic view, equation method , such as gathering the kind of sale and price their information, it may help the seller measure whether it ought set up how much sale price to the product to let many consumers feel the most reasonable in order to increase its sale number in the country's consumption market.

On conclusion, consumer behavior measurement, micro economic method is more suitable or acceptable to compare macro economic method in any countries' consumption market nowadays.

Economic methods measure crime behavior

when and how and why cases

CHAPTER EIGHT

Unemployment causes crime

Why does global macro economic environment become worse, it will bring many countries' unemployment rates raise as well as it can cause crime rate number rises in possible? I believe that they have case and effect relationship. In most countries, unemployment is higher today than it was in the 1960s. Why are these such large variations in unemployment, it brings more crime after 1960s? I shall indicate the reasons as below:

(1) Hiring costs raise unemployment as firms become more anxious to keep the workers they have,which puts upward pressure on wages. So, when the global societies employers feel any costs are increasing after 1960s, e.g. manufacturing cost, rent cost, office and/or office electricity cost , goods transportation cost , even wage cots etc. hen, many employers will choose to dismiss many workers and unemployment rate will be raised. When many workers lose jobs for long time. Social crime number will increase, in special, the low educational and low skillful workers. Their crime mind and crime behaviors will be caused by long term unemployment.

(2) Generous unemployment benefits may make workers more selective in their job search and raise unemployment. IN fact, after 1960s, global macro economic environment had been improving from manufacturing industry to service, than high technological industries development both. It will cause the developing countries, such as Africa, China, Hong Kong, Korea etc., their low education and low skillful workers lose jobs suddenly, due to their manufacturing skills won't be popular needed to employers. For example, old cloth drwssing machines will be replaced from new high technological cloth dressing machines, old car manufacturing factory method will be replaced by high technological artificial intelligent car manufacturing method. When the low manufacturing skillful workers can not find any manufacturing jobs to match their manufactury skills in their job search process. Then, in long term unemployment situation, the high

technolobical development factor will cause the low manufacturing skillful workers have crime or anti-social psychological mind to cause crime behaviors easily.

(3) Mismatch between worker skills and labor demand means that unemployed workers have differenties competing for jobs which will raise the level of unemployment. Similiar , due to global macro economic environment changes, e.g. many high technological skillful workers number increases, but the supply of high technological skillful workers number can not grow rapidly. So, it brings the shortage of high technological skillful labor supply. Otherwise, in global societies , many low technological skillful workers, they do not continue to learn any kinds of high technological knowledge to prepare to find any high technological jobs easily. So, global societies bring the mismatch between worker skills and labor demand. Consequently, it many bring many low technological skillful workers still lose jobs for long time , Then, their crime behaviors will also be influenced to raise in possible.

(4) Lacking a well-functioning education system and active labor market policy could potentialy raise mismatch and unemployed. The reason is easy to understand. For Hong Kong example, HK crime rate is increasing after 1960s. although, HK's manufacturing industry is replaced by monetary, service industries maninly nowadays. HK lacks a well functioning education system to educate the low educational level and low skillful youngers to be trained their skills to prepare to do further high technological development industry. So, HK's social weakness is a lack of high technological jobs well-functioning education system. It can train many youngers to do high technological jobs in active labor market.

Nowadays, HK has many employers need high technolgical workers in active labor market. It will cause many HK high technological businesses can not find any high technological workers easily in HK. Then, they will choose to find overseas high technological workers to replace HK domestic workers, as well as it will cause HK high technological workers' wages to be reduced. Otherwise, overseas high technological workers‘ wages will be raised . Even longer time , HK many high technological workers will lose jobs, because their skills can be replaced from overseas high technological workers easily. If their demand still need HK employers raise their salaries to compare to overseas high technological workers' salaries . Due to this global macro high technological workers demand increasing factor influences to HK, so China, or other developing high technological job markets. Then, it may cause many developing countries' high technological workers lose thier jobs, due to the developed countries' high technological workers can be replaced to do their job more easy, even their salaries demand is lower to compare to the developing countries high technological workers' salaries demand. So, when the developing countries ' high technological workers feel unfair, they lose jobs, due to overseas developed countries' high technological wotkers are replaced. It will cause that they will choose to do crime behavior in society more easier.

Also, HK's job security legislation is poor to comapre Western countries. For example, US, UK, New Zealand, Australia etc. Western countries. They have good citizen security legislation. All those Western countries' citizen own unemployment assistance, when they lose jobs to do in long time or they unemploy long time. Then, they have authority to need their governments to give unemployment assistance. If they have no any unemployment or they have less unemployment before 60 or 65 retirement age. Then, after 60 or 65 age, their government will still give them money for life assistance per week, till to they die. Otherwise, HK government only have job security legislation to reduce employee individual 5% of salary for MPF (mututary provident fund) and employee's 5 % salary for MPF maximum per month for their retirement benefit. HK government won't give HK citizen money for life assistance after 65 retirement age. If the HK citizen earned less salary before 65 age, then it is not enough to provide social welfare assistance to any HK citizen after they reach 65 age in possible. So, it explains that why some HK old people will do crime behaviors more easily.

Does long-term unemployment cause social problem? There is no question that high unemployment is a major social problem, but zero unemployment is neither feasible nor a desirable object for poicy. In fact, it is natural and acceptable that some workers are unemployed between different jobs. For example, when one waiter is dismisses or unemployed , due to his restaurant employer loses business or another waiter is employed different reasons . Then, he spends more six months to seek the same waiter job, but he still can not find any same job easily. Then, he chooses to learn any similar waiter service skills, e.g. hotel waiter service skill. He needs to spend another six months to lean the new hotel waiter service and attitude knowledge, because restaurant waiter service skil is very diffeent to hotel waiter service skill need. He needs to learn how to serve hotel restaurant clients. Thus, in this year unemployment minimum period, it includes the six months seeling restaurant waiter job period and another six months learning hotel waiter job learing period, this restaurant waiter unemployed worker won;t earn any salary in this year. It means that long-term unemployment period to this career seeker. Also, it is rational for this restaurant waiter unemployed worker not to take the first restaurant waiter job, he can get , but to attempt to learn hotel restaurant waiter service knowledge to wait for a hotel restaurant waiter job employment in possible, where he can use his specific competence and be rewarded for this with a reasonable waiter occupation wage.

If this restaurant unemployed waiter was occasionally unemployed for a few weeks between jobs, this is not necessarily a big social problem. The really serious socal problem occurs when workers are stuck in unemployment for many months or even years, such as this restaurant unemployed waiter case, he has one year unemployment period at least. It includes, the six months without salary restaurant waiter job search period and another six months without hotel restuarant waiter learning period. Moreover, he also need to pay tuition for this hotel restaurant waiter course as well as he also needs to pass the practice and paper test of hotel restaurant waiter course in order to earn this certificate of their hotel restaurant waiter occupation and he can find any hotel restaurant waiter job more easy. However, if he can not pass this course, then he needs to do choice either paying tuition to study this course again or he can attempt to find the same past restaurant waiter job again or he can attempt to learn another new skill to further change his new occupation career. Then , it brings this question : Does long term unemployment cause or influence this restaurant waiter perform crime behavior in society ? I believe that the answer is depended that how long in typical worker will be unemployed. To see what determines the expected duration of unemployment , assume for simplicity that workers who find a job in a particular month start working at the end of that month, so that all workers who become unemployed remain unemployed for least one month. So, the duration of unemployment depends on three factors as well as these three factors can influence any unemployed workers choose to do crime behaviors in society more easily. They include as below:

(1) Whether the country is a higher rate or lower rate of unemployment in society means , that there are more workers competing for available jobs in the country and less chance to find a jon, which needs a longer duration of unemployment. For Hong Kong employment market example, nowadays, there are many young people (university students) choose to

study monetary subject to do bank jobs, or seek further monetary , share investment monetary related occupations to work. Hence, there are more monetary related subject, e.g. finance, accounting university graduate students compete for any available monetary related jobs in HK, but in fact, HK monetary related investment jobs number is not enough or supply shortage.

It depends on macro economic environment whether there are many overseas investors choose to set up their businesses in HK or there are less overseas investors choose to set up their businesses in HK. So, if the year, there was less overseas investors number in HK. Then , it may cause any kinds of monetary related jobs number as less to supply in HK job market. If the year, there were a many monetary subject graduate students increased. It causes the effect of a longer duration of unemployment to the year monetary subject university graduate students in HK. Then, the any related monetary crime cases may also increase , due to these HK monetary subject university students can not find any monetary related jobs in HK easily. They do not want to find other jobs to replace monetary jobs, it may be due to low salary is paid, unsatisfactory workin environment, without monetary job duties practice chance satisfies their further career development need. If HK macro economic environment was continue poor after the year. It kept to two year, threee years, even more than five years poor macro economic period. Then, the overseas investors number to HK will decrease, even many HK overseas investors also planned to forgive their businesses to be close in HK. It means that they choose to close their HK businesses and their offices were left. Then, it will influence any HK monetary related jobs number will reduce, but as the same time every year, HK monetary major subject unviersity students number is also increasing. Consequently, it will cause or influence any kinds of monetary crime cases will be increased to HK by the long term unemployment to many HK university major monetary subject graduate students factor.

(2) A high rate of separations (people leaving jobs) means that there are more job opening, so the duration of unemployment decreases. It means that when the country has there working people often change old jobs or they planned to find new jobs to replace current jobs or they expect to change another new jobs reasons. It implies that the country's economy is improving or better to compare before. There are more job openings, many employers create different kinds of new jobs to satisfy their businesses needs. So the duration of unemployment will be influenced to decrease

in possible. Because many new creative jobs number is caused. Working people have much chance to attempt to find another new jobs to replace their current jobs in the country.

Even, some working people are doing one job, which can give reasonable wage and it can have more promotion chance in this current job. They will still choose to find another new jobs , it may be that they feel there are many new creative jobs , which can bring new exciting feeling, which can bring nre exciting feeing , more satisfactory feeling , more fun feeling , more successful feeling, more interesting feeling to compare their current jobs . So, it is not only higher salary factor to influence them to change current jobs.

For US job market example, US macro economic environment has been improving very good, many new creative jobs are increasing, e.g. in (AI) job aspect, artificial intelligence scientist , (AI) engineer, big data gathering scientist, non-manual automatic (AI) controlling worker, e.g. artificial intelligence factory machine controlling workers, in medicine job aspect, e.g. drug researcher, DNA cell science researcher, brain doctor, occupational psychological doctor, space science researcher or space scientist etc. creative occupations. There new creative occupations can supply enough jobs to many US high educational level graduate students and they can encourage them to change their current more easily.

In fact, US , these are many different occupations, scientists have jobs, they are doing, but they still expect or plan to change another new similar or different new creative jobs easily. Because the US high education new creative science jobs supply number is more than the US any science graduate students number in US labor market nowadays. So, it explains that why US crime number is decreasing nowadays. Because US has good macro economic environment. US itself country's any new creative job supply number and non creative job supply number must have more than the US graduate student number every year. So, US has good macro economic environment to supply enough jobs number to any US low educational and high educating level young people to job.

Consequently, it causes crime number reduced in US society nowadays. Otherwisem HK has less creative jobs to be supplied to let HK young university graduate students, as well as HK university graduate students number is increasing, but university level jobs number is decreasing at this moment. So, it explains that only HK society increases crime number easily nowadays.

All of above analysis, I assume that the standard measure of long term unemployment id the number of workers who have been unemployed for more than 12 months as well as they feel worry to earn enough income to support their basic essential needs, such as eating need, living need, but it excludes non essential needs, such as entertainment need, travelling need, education need.

So, when these countries young people feel long time unemployment to cause they can not have enough income to support their basic essential needs, then It may influence they choose to do crime behaviors in themselves societies more easily. I shall indicate how any why high turnover and low turnover countries will bring high or low crome behavioral causes in some countries themselves societies.

OECD(2011) concluded the high turnover countries, abourt 10 % of unemployment is long term . So it brings low crime rate . Otherwise, in the low turnover countries, 30 to 60% of the unemployed have beed out of jobs for more than one year, it will bring high crime rate. It explains that it has direct relationship between crime rate number and unemployment rate more than one year number from the average 1999 to 2008 more or less than one year unemployment rate statistics. It indicates that the average 1999 to 2008 period, these low turnover countries have high unemployment rate more than a year , then these low turnover countries crime rate will be influenced to increase also, these low turnvoer or high unemployment countries include: Turkey, France, Netherlands, Greece, Cyech Republic, Hungery, Slovall Republic, Germany, Italy, Portugal, Belgium, Poland, Spain, Switerland, Ireland, Finland, Austia, Japan, United Kingdom. So , these countries' crime rare has been increasing in this period. Otherwise, these high turnover countries or low unemployment rare more than one year, then these high turnover countries crime rate will be influenced to decrease also. There high turnover or low unemployment countries include: Iceland, Norway, United States, Mexico, New Zealand, Canada, Denmark, Australia, Sweden.

In conclusion, it explains that when the country's macro economy environment is improved of better, then it has more high education or low education level jobs to be supplied to let many young people have any kinds of jobs to work easily. Them, it will bring low unemployment effect and low crime rate effect both . Consequently, unemployment has relationship to cause crime rate rises or reduced in possible in any countries' societies.

Reference

OECD , employment and labor market statistics, OECD , 27 April 2011. source http://www.oecdilibrary.org/statistics.

CHAPTER NINE

Relationship between a recession and crime

Has it relationship between a recession and crime? To answer this relationship question, I shall explain what is macroeconomics. Then, you will give more clear understanding why and why recession will impact social crime behaviors to bre rasied in possible.

What is Macroeconomics? Macroeconomics is a branch of economics that studies how the aggregate economy behaves. In macroeconomics, economy-wide
phenomena are examined such as inflation, price levels, rate of economic growth, national income, gross domestic product
(GDP), and changes in unemployment.On the other hand, microeconomics looks at the behavior of individual actors in an economy (like people, households, industries, etc).
Macroeconomics is the branch of economics that deals with the structure, performance, behavior,and decision-making of the whole, or aggregate, economy, instead of focusing on individual markets.The two main areas of macroeconomic study are long term economic growth and shorter term business cycles.

There are two sides to the study of economics: macroeconomics and microeconomics. As the term implies,
macroeconomics looks at the overall, big picture scenario of the economy. Put simply, it focuses on the way the economy performs as a whole, and then analyzes how different sectors of the economy relate to one another to understand how the economy functions. This includes looking at variables like unemployment, GDP, and inflation.

Macroeconomists develop models explaining relationships between these factors. Such macroeconomic models, and the forecasts they produce, are used by government entities to aid in the construction and evaluation of economic policy, by businesses to set strategy in domestic and global markets, and by investors to predict and plan for movements in various asset markets.

Given the enormous scale of government budgets and the impact of economic policy on consumers and businesses, macroeconomics clearly concerns itself with significant issues. Properly applied, economic theories can offer
illuminating insights on how economies function and the long-term consequences of particular policies and decisions. Macroeconomic theory can also help individual businesses and investors make better decisions through a more thorough understanding of what motivates other parties and how to best maximize utility and scarce resources.It is also important to understand the limitations of economic theory. Theories are often created in a vacuum and lack
certain real-world details like taxation, regulation and transaction costs. The real world is also decidedly complicated and their matters of social preference and conscience that do not lend themselves to mathematical analysis.

Even with the limits of economic theory, it is important and worthwhile to follow the major macroeconomic indicators like GDP,
inflation and unemployment. The performance of companies, and by extension their stocks, is significantly influenced by the economic
conditions in which the companies operate and the study of macroeconomic statistics can help an investor make better decisions and spot turning points.

● Specific Areas of Crime rate increasing ,due to poor macro economy environment influences

Macroeconomics is a rather broad field, but two specific areas of research are representative of this discipline. The first area
is the factors that determine long-term economic growth, or increases in the national income. The other involves the causes and

consequences of short-term fluctuations in national income and employment, also known as the business cycle, such as researching whether recession will cause crime rate rising issue.

Economic growth refers to an increase in aggregate production in an economy. Macroeconomists study economic growth with an eye toward understanding the factors that either promote or retard economic growth in order to support economic policies that will
support growth, development, and rising living standards. Growth is commonly modeled as a function of physical capital, human capital, labor force, and technology. So, when economic growth is raising, then unemployment rate will decrease in possible.

- Business Positive or negative Cycles and
the country's macro economic environment is good and bad relationship

A long term macroeconomic growth trends, the levels and rates-of-change of major macroeconomic variables such as
employment and national output go through occasional fluctuations up or down, expansions and recessions, in a phenomenon known as the business cycle.

- Macroeconomics vs. Microeconomics , what can influence crime rate more?

Macroeconomics differs from microeconomics, which focuses on smaller factors that affect choices made by individuals and companies.Factors studied in both microeconomics and macroeconomics typically have an influence on one another. For example, the unemployment
level in the economy as a whole has an effect on the supply of workers from which a company can hire.

A key distinction between micro and macroeconomics is that macroeconomic aggregates can sometimes behave in ways that are very different or even the opposite of the way that analogous microeconomic variables do.Meanwhile, microeconomics looks at economic tendencies, or what can happen when individuals make certain choices. Individuals are typically classified into subgroups, such as buyers, sellers, and business owners. These actors interact with each other according to the laws of supply and demand for resources, using money and interest rates as pricing mechanisms for coordination

- What factors Cause of recessions ?

A recession implies a fall in real GDP. An official definition of a recession is a period of negative economic growth for two consecutive quarters. Recessions are

primarily caused by a fall in aggregate demand (AD).

This demand-side shock could be due to several factors, such as

· A financial crisis. If banks have a shortage of liquidity, they reduce lending – this reduces investment

· A rise in interest rates – increases the cost of borrowing and reduces demand

· Fall in asset prices. – negative wealth effect leads to less spending

· Fall in consumer/business confidence also exacerbated by negative multiplier effect.

· Appreciation in exchange rate – exports less competitive

· Fiscal austerity – when government cuts spending

Recessions can also be caused by

· Supply-side shock, e.g. rise in oil prices cause inflation and lower spending power.

For example, in US, bank failures led to a fall in the money supply and deflationary pressures.Bank failures also caused lost confidence and discourage investment.

· Negative multiplier effect – initial fall in spending caused a knock on effect throughout the economy.

There were no automatic stabilisers. People were made unemployed and so started spending less themselves. For example , causes of UK recessions1981 recession was caused by:

1.High value of the pound which made exports more expensive and reduced demand for exports.This recession particularly impacted on British manufacturing. The Pound soared due to the discovery of North Sea Oil but also the high interest rates.

2.High-interest rates. In 1979, inflation in the UK was over 15%. The new Conservative government was committed to reducing high inflation they inherited. They pursued a tight monetary policy (higher interest rates) and tight fiscal policy (higher taxes, lower government spending. This reduced inflation but at the cost of falling spending, investment and output.interest-rates.

3.Tight Fiscal Policy. To control inflation the government were committed to reducing the levels of Government borrowing.
This was influenced by Monetarist beliefs that controlling excess government borrowing was essential to the economy. Therefore the government increased taxes which reduced the disposable income of consumers and therefore reduced consumer spending.

A recession occurs when there is a fall in economic growth for two consecutive quarters. However, if growth is very low there will be increased spare capacity and increased unemployment; people will feel there is a recession. A key feature in determining the rate of economic growth is the level of consumer and business confidence. If confidence was high then higher interest rates may not reduce demand. However if confidence is low and people fear they may be made unemployed, then they will start spending less, causing AD to fall (or increase at a slower rate). Therefore this shows that expectations are very important and it is possible for "people to talk themselves into a recession".

For an important feature of the UK economy is international trade case. Therefore the UK would be affected by a global recession. For example, a recession in the EU would cause a fall in demand for UK exports reducing our AD (EU accounts for 60% of our trade, therefore, is important). Also, a recession in other countries would affect economic confidence if people see the US in a recession they are worried and will spend less. However, a global recession may not cause a recession in the UK if domestic demand remains high.

Classical economists believe that any fall in Real GDP will be temporary and will end when labour markets adjust to the new price level. Classical economists argue that if there is a fall in AD then, in the short term, there will be a fall in real GDP However in the great depression of 1930s Keynes was very critical of this classical view he said that the long period of negative growth showed that markets do not automatically clear he argued that this was for various reasons.

1.Wages are sticky downwards. Firms should cut wages to reflect lower prices but in reality, workers are very resistant to cuts in nominal wages.

2.If wages were cut in response to unemployment, workers would have less spending power, therefore AD would continue
to fall.

● Can economic crises bring rise in crime ?

Crime may peak during economic crises,
During periods of economic stress, the incidence of robbery may double, and homicide and motor vehicle theft also increase.While a consistent relationship between specific crimes and specific economic factors could not be established, the evidence shows that crime is linked to the economic climate. Such findings are consistent with criminal motivation theory, which suggests that economic stress causes an increase in criminal behaviour. The available data do not, however, support the theory of criminal opportunity, which suggests that decreased levels of production and consumption may reduce some types of crime, such as property crime, by creating fewer potential crime targets."The presence of youth gangs, the availability of weapons and potential targets, drug and alcohol consumption and the effectiveness of law enforcement all play a significant role in enabling or restraining overall crime levels",

● Relationship between a recession and crime

Criminologists say bad economies create more crime; economists say the opposite. But recent data reveals neither explanation is right.

I've been wondering if hard economic times would cause people to commit more crimes.

For example, areas with chronic poverty and unemployment tend to have high rates of child neglect and abuse. Child neglect and abuse greatly increase the risk of juveniles getting involved in crime.So areas with high rates of unemployment cop a double whammy. Their crime rates are higher because of the direct effect of unemployment and its long-term indirect effects as well.

Will the current recession produce an increase in crime? If the recession doesn't last long, there may be no effect at all.

But if the recession is deep and the pool of young long-term unemployed rises, there is every reason to expect an increase in crime.

Moreover, if this happens, the effects may last a long while. The longer you are out of work, the harder it is to find a job, and the more attractive crime becomes as an alternative source of income. And what happens this recession depends on still more factors, the most important being the income that can be earned from crime e.g.selling illegal drugs. Many thoughtful observers think that we put too many offenders in prison for too long. For some criminals, such as low-level drug dealers and former inmates returned to prison for parole violations, that may be so. The difference results not from willingness to send convicted offenders to prison in many countries' legal system

● May Economic crises trigger rise in crime ?

For the same offense, you will spend more time in prison here than in England. Canada has seen roughly the same decline in crime,
but its imprisonment rate has been relatively flat for at least two decades. Another possible reason for reduced crime is that potential
victims may have become better at protecting themselves by equipping their homes with burglar alarms, installing extra locks on their cars, and moving into safer buildings or even safer neighborhoods.

We have only the faintest idea, however, about how common these trends are or what effects on crime they may have. Are their crime behaviors caused by economic crises ?
How to explain complex link between recession and crime? For In the Environmental Protection Agency example, required oil companies to stop putting lead in gasoline. At the same time, lead in paint was banned for any new home though old buildings still have lead paint, which children can absorb.

● Why do recessions at labour market entry matter for crime? So, why is it that youth who graduate during recessions are more likely to engage in crime?

Those who leave school during a recession, when youth unemployment rates are particularly high, struggle to find a job but do not yet have financial insurance. Knock-on effects can then lead to criminal careers for the young. On the other hand, those who have criminal records early on in their career may reduce their job opportunities and expected returns in the legal labour market see. However , I agree that crime is not only a feature of the teenage years — crime rates decrease with age but do not disappear subsequently. That suggests that there is an initial effect but criminal activity is somewhat persistent over the life cycle.

● Can that persistence be explained by the long-term impact of recessions?

A typical recession leads to a 5 percentage points higher than normal unemployment rate.What is the long-term impact of graduating into such conditions? Our empirical analysis of the link between crime and unemployment at labour market entry is based on a variety of US and UK cohort and individual level data sources. We exploit cohort level data

for both countries to estimate the average effect of initial labour market conditions on criminal activity of cohorts that enter the labour market at different points
in time, taking into account differences in cohort composition.

- Is crime Rates increasing during recessions?

A recession is a significant decline in economic activity spread across the economy, lasting more than a few months, normally visible in production, employment, real income, and other indicators. A recession begins when the economy reaches a peak of. Have they the relationship between economic indicators and crime rates in terms of whether there is a correlation between a given indicator and crime? A positive correlation exists when increases in one variable are accompanied by increases in another variable. A negative correlation, on the other hand, occurs when increases in one variable are accompanied by decreases in another variable.

One important concept is the idea that correlation does not imply causation; the presence of two sets of data (two variables) showing similar trends does not indicate that changes in one variable cause any visible changes in the other. Instead, a correlation shows that changes in one variable can, to some extent, predict changes in another variable. For instance, while some neighborhoods may exhibit a relationship between certain types of crime and the economy, other neighborhoods may exhibit a relationship between different types of crime and the economy or may not exhibit a relationship at all.

Consequently, researchers tend to use individual economic indicators, such as the unemployment rate, as a proxy for the state of the economy. However, any given indicator may not be generalizable to the state of the economy as a whole during any one given recession or across recessions.Despite the limitations in using specific economic variables as proxies for a complex economic state, this methodology does allow researchers to isolate variables and analyze their individual.Generalizability is typically defined as the extent to which the results generated by a variable being studied can be applied to other settings, times, or groups of subjects and be expected to deliver a similar outcome. Specifically, during the most recent economic downturn, many referred to the
unemployment rate and the proportion of home foreclosures as proxies for economic health.

- What are the real factors cause the changes in the crime rates?

Impact of Unemployment on Crime

the unemployment rate is one of the most widely referenced economic indicators. In discussions of potential impacts of the economy on crime rates, many scholars and policy makers use the unemployment rate as a proxy for economic strength. Congress has shown interest in the relationship between the economy—unemployment, in particular—and crime rates since the 1970s. The most recent recession, which was accompanied by a rise in the unemployment rate, once again focused attention on the relationship between unemployment and crime rates.

Researchers and scholars have several theories concerning the relationship between

unemployment and crime. One of these theories, the economic theory of crime, assumes that people make rational choices between legitimate activities and criminal activities as a source of economic gain. More specifically, the comparison is between the economic benefit of legitimate work versus that of violent or property crime, after accounting for crime-related costs such as incarceration. Although the theory was originally formulated with an application to all crimes, many researchers have used it in discussions of unemployment and property crime. This theory predicts a positive correlation between unemployment and property crime; in other words, that increases in the unemployment rate will be correlated with increases in property crime rates. The reason for this positive correlation, according to the economic model, is that during periods when there are fewer opportunities for legitimate income, people may turn to illegal activities, while when more jobs are available, the risks of committing a crime may be weighed against the opportunity for legitimate work.

Were a direct link between unemployment and the property crime rate, varying one would

necessarily vary the other? The lack of conclusive evidence for a strong, or even significant,correlation between the two suggests that the unemployment rate may have an indirect relationship with the property crime rate. Although unemployment is correlated with overall economic conditions, it may not fully capture other key economic indicators such as work hours, employment stability, and wages. Some researchers, for example, have found that employment stability and wages may correlate more strongly with the property crime rate than does unemployment.

CHAPTER TEN

Economic Theories of Crime

What is economic theories of crime ?This brief literature review highlights three key economic frameworks that can be used to explain a persistent social problem
in modern society, crime and delinquency: the rational model, the present-oriented or myopic model, and the radical political
economic model. Based on a cost-benefit analysis, an individuals decision to engage in crime in the rational model is consistent
in the short-and long-term. Present-oriented individuals, however, focus on the short-term benefits without particular concern
for the long-term consequences of their actions. The radical political economic model focuses on the following key political and socio-economic factors that sustain crime: relative deprivation, poverty and inequality, unemployment, and class conflict.The conclusion includes a conceptual map integrating the three frameworks.

Some economists and crime psychologists believe that crime is not limited to certain areas or to certain socioeconomic classes
of society. Criminal activities take many forms, including theft, homicide,assault, fraud, embezzlement, and blackmail. So why does crime persist? Are there underlying factors that can explain criminal behavior? Can we lower
the incentives for criminal behavior? Do criminals take opportunity costs of committing a crime into account? The social science field has long been interested in these questions.

This literature review focuses on the discipline of economics and its assumptions about individual decisions to commit crime. The standard assumption
is that individuals who commit crimes are rational decision makers who expect to gain something from criminal activity, and this gain is greater than

the expected costs associated with being caught. Most of the research in this area focuses on the effects of incentives to engage in criminal behavior and on the use of cost-benefit analysis to assess alternative policies to reduce crime. However, not all crime can be categorized as rational behavior. Socioeconomic factors are also assumed to affect crime, and alternative theories to explain criminal activities are used to challenge the standard assumption of rational behavior.

The main objective of this review is to identify the key economic frameworks that are used to explain crime and delinquency. The three key frameworks include the rational model of crime, the present-oriented or myopic model of crime, and the radical political economic model of crime.

Economists have begun to question whether the standard assumption of rational behavior holds when consideringwhy individuals engage in criminal activity. Can we really assume that all criminals make rational decisions to commit a crime? Individual preferences, psychic factors, and other motivations for crime may play an equally large role in explaining crime. However these factors are much harder to incorporate into economic models of crime. Hence, there is limited empirical research in this area. It will be interesting to see how the growing field of behavioral economics can help to explain crime and delinquency.

The three main economic models of crime are the rationa lmodel, the present oriented or myopic model, and the radical political economic model. Each model emphasizes different factors that influence individual decisions to commit crime and different ways of combating crime. What is the Rational Model of Crime mean?

Economics can be defined as a discipline that studies how scarce resources are allocated by the forces of supply and demand to meet different needs in society. In the same way, economists argue that crime is a result of individuals' making choices between using their scarce resources of time and effort in legitimate or in illegitimate activities. A key assumption is that when making these choices, individuals are rational and choose the best option based on the available information and resources. Individuals are perceived to be promoting their self-interest by rationally selecting options that provide them with the greatest benefits that are expected to exceed the costs associated with these options.

The profit from crime is traditionally measured in terms of monetary benefits but can also include physical, psychic, and other benefits. The "punishment" or costs of crime include the risk of detection, apprehension, and conviction and the severity of punishment. Economists do not refute that environmental, psychological, and biological factors may affect criminal activity. Nevertheless, they argue that individuals are free to choose between different courses of options available to them. Therefore, as long as there is a rational element of choice available, individuals who decide to commit a crime will react to changes in the probability of apprehension and the

severity of punishment .This framework leads to a key concept, namely, the "opportunity cost" of crime. Any decision that involves a choice between two or more options has an opportunity cost. An opportunity cost can be defined as the value of the next best alternative within the context of making a decision. Put differently, an opportunity cost can be viewed as the benefits an individual could have received by taking an alternative decision or action. In essence, the true cost of crime for a potential criminal is the opportunity cost of spending time in prison. The opportunity cost varies among individuals

irrespective of the length of incarceration.

The rational framework distinguishes between static and dynamic models of crime. In a static model, individuals compare the costs and benefits of engaging in crime in a single time period. In a dynamic model, the individual

considers multiple time periods. Decisions made in the past, for example, impact the decision-making process in the present.

● Is Unemployment caused crime by poor macro economy environment factor?

Different models examine the different relationships between unemployment and crime. Some economic models assume that unemployment either lowers the opportunity costs of crime or that it increases

the need to supplement income from sources other than legal employment. However, how do individuals form expectations about their earnings potential in the labor market? If there is a considerable gap between what the individual believes is attainable (group experience) and what is

unattainable
(larger society experience), an individual perceives this gap as relative deprivation. Hence the opportunity costs of crime may be reduced because the returns from regular employment are seen as minimal. In contrast, if the larger society also suffers from unemployment, the shortage of employment opportunities may still be considered equitable. attention that crimes, such as burglary or theft, receive in comparison with white collar crime, although the latter type of crimes represent a larger
proportion of monetary losses than the former type.

Crime accompanies social life from its very beginning – it occurs in every society and in every stage of its development, regardless of its structure, system or historical period. Undoubtedly, crime is a consequence of many social and economic problems which
constantly change, therefore there are so many controversial and unresolved issued connected with the influence of social and economical factors on crime. This article is an attempt to find an answer to whether the socio-economic factors clearly have a substantial impact on
crime.

Regardless of whether we like it or not – crime is a constant component of our life. The crime level is influenced by lots of factors
which nature is heterogeneous. Among them, we may distinguish the socio - economic situation of the offender. Statistics (not only Polish) seem to confirm the assumption that there is a strong connection between social and economic conditions and the level of crime .

● SOCIO - ECONOMIC FACTORS CAUSES
CRIME RATE INCREASES

Crime and changes in the structure of crime are both affected by such elements as: the degree of economic development, socio - political system that functions in a given country, the progress of industrialization and urbanization, transformations in social structure which are age-related to members of the society and finally, migrations. Transformations may be carried out in a revolutionary way or throughout
a longer period of time, they can also occur suddenly as a result of some turbulent changeovers and rapid changes which happen in a given community.

In the case of our country one should consider political changes, accompanied by destabilizing and disintegrative processes, political changes with the transition from a communist to a democratic regime. Further modifications were related to the economic system, changes in ownership structure and the emergence of structural unemployment .New conditions caused a shift in social structure, namely, new social groups were formed, social hierarchy was changed, and many social groups suffered economic degradation.

● The influence of socio - economic factors on crime

Therefore, one should ask a question whether in fact the economic situation shapes the level of crime rate . While being under constant modifications and transformations, society will never stay unchanged. Changes in the number, gender, age structure, migration (demographic changes) also have their mutual influence related to the economy, system of power, education, health protection, religion, and crime. Poor economic situation may translate into crime by an increase in unemployment. It should be noted that unemployment, naturally connected with the economy may have a different dimension. We distinguish between the structural, cyclical, long-term, and frictional unemployment. Because of the social and demographic factors, such as gender, age or education level of people affected by the unemployment, there may be various relationships and impact on criminal activity.An analysis of police statistics shows that the highest intensity of crime occurs among unemployed people who are under thirty years of age . If an individual is affected by long-term unemployment, he or she starts to be affected by the consequences of such a situation, namely a sense of exclusion, injustice, and finally the lack of hope of finding a legitimate source of income . The analysis shows that unemployment brings on crime against property rather than violence . However, it should be noted that the increase in unemployment in various ways may affect particular social groups by increasing or decreasing their criminal activity. At this point one should outline four specific relationships between unemployment and crime as below:

· Some offenders combine their legal professional work with criminal activity. Legal business is treated as a camouflage for illegal operation. In this case, the development of unemployment may reduce the “gray zone” business, as the legal work, in this case, gives a sense of security for conducting criminal activity.

· There is a number of crimes, possible to be committed only during conducting activities while being legally employed, for example: "handing over bribes to officials", "employee theft". In those situations the growth of unemployment will inhibit the number of crimes of the above mentioned type, rather than increase them.

· Young people, in particular distinguish between two options: being legally employed, or being involved in a criminal activity. If the lack of work prevails, the willingness to take an income from illegal sources may be decisive. Unemployment, in this perspective may cause an increase in crime.

· There are people for whom unemployment is strictly related to their living style. This group of people treat legal work as an abnormal situation – those people are not part of the labor market. For them, the lack of employment is part of their cultural identity, and criminal activity is, in their environment, a socially accepted source of income. In this case, an increase in unemployment will have no influence on the formation of criminal behavior.

Further analysis of inter-relations of factors related to the discussed problem may incline to believe that in a period of an economic recession, a higher level of crime against property and lower against the person is being observed, whereas, during a period of prosperity (an economic boom) the situation is
other way round: higher level of crime against the person and lower against property is being distinguished. Apart from unemployment other economic factors such as: poverty, the level, dynamics and diversity of earnings and the pace of economic development influence the crime rate. Poverty has long been the factor which has been strongly associated with criminal activity. As it was indicated by Alain Peyrefitte, "crime is the child of poverty".

While trying to explain the influence of socio - economic changes on crime, a number of changes in the economic system should be taken into account, such as the emergence of
economic crises, periods of economic prosperity, the processes of European unification, EU enlargement, globalization, the processes of industrialization and urbanization. If the economic components affect almost all types of social activity, there must be a link between them and the crime. Conditions, economic tension may create some situations, often stressful situations that may facilitate criminal activity . Initially, the

analysis of the relationship between social and economic transformation and changes in the crime indicated that there is a causal connection, but now this assumption is not so obvious. One may only unquestionably talk about correlation between a group of various factors, also non-economical and certain types of crime. A good economic situation, a period of prosperity may both influence either increase or decrease in the number of offenses.

First of all, it may increase the possibility to commit a crime as the easiness and availability of products make them an easy target for a thief or even a person who has a desire to steal an item without really the need to have it. Abundance of goods cause that products may become an object of a crime (e.g become vandalized). Furthermore, if people have too much leisure, they tend to change their lifestyle – and this change is associated with taking part in or participate in events or actions with other people. This causes a greater opportunity for people to be involved in a prohibited actions and crimes against the person. A period of prosperity may, on the other hand decrease the possibility to commit a crime as people stick to generally accepted social standards and the desire to commit an illegal actions e.g. theft, swindle is reduced. They feel more socially secured and safe. The better social and economic status people have, the lower need to be involved in something prohibited by law. In case of a well-paid job, also motivational elements appear as well as the fear of the consequences of a wrongful act. In literature of this field, there is no evidence that there is a connection between the level of crime and the level of industrialization. However, there is a strong connection between the level of crime and spatial mobility of the population, and the size of migration.

The internationalization of crime causes intensification of organized crime. Possibilities to commit a crime also change – smuggling, tax frauds, economic crime, production of drugs and weapon, money frauds, prostitution, ?money laundering", customs offenses, corruption. The changing structure of crime, its forms and ways of committing it indicate a real change in social structure and transformations of the social life as well as missing norms and values of societies which in a given historical period may be observed.

In conclusion,the discussed and analyzed socio - economic factors incline to believe that social and economical sphere of human life is interrelated and interdependent. There are certain correlations with the crime level and social behavior as well as with economy and human vulnerability to commit an offense. However, careful The influence of socio - economic factors on crime examination in this respect is still needed. Causal dependencies which occur in societies on every stage of their development are difficult to explain.So how to carry out on the research, analysis of recovery plans and criminal statistics as well as literature allowed to form a conclusion that people should not only focus on individuals in crime prevention programs but on such forms of activity that would be targeted to whole societies. Preventive measures should aim at reducing both economic and social inequalities, e.g balance the level of income or promote social cohesion. Although various crime preventive strategies and programs continue to be developed , they may only reduce crime rate on a small scale, basically they will not have a clear influence on the increase or decrease in a criminal activity in a particular country or in a global dimension as too many social and economic factors should be taken into account.

CHAPTER ELEVEN

Is poor macro economic environment a main root to crime causation

Is poor macro economic environment cause crime essentially? Economic Theories indicate the roots of crime are diverse and a discipline like economics, predicated on rational behavior, may be at something of a disadvantage in explaining a phenomenon largely viewed as irrational. A recent survey suggests that three general issues are of central concern in the economics of crime literature: the effects of incentives on criminal behavior, how decisions interact in a market-setting, and the use of cost-benefit analysis to assess alternative policies to reduce crime will focus on the role of incentives on criminal behavior.

However, trend in criminal participation rates in most industrialized economies is a difficult task. Many social scientists argue that crime is closely related to work, education and poverty and that truancy, youth unemployment and crime are by products or even measures of social exclusion. "Blue-collar"criminals often have limited education and possess limited labor market skills. These characteristics partly explain the poor employment records and low legitimate earnings of most criminals. These sort of issues originally led economists to examine the relationship between wages and unemployment rates on crime. More recently economists have also considered the benefits and costs of educational programs to reduce crime.

A related question concerns the impact of sanctions. For example, does increased imprisonment lower the crime rate? How does the deterrent effect of formal sanctions arise? Although criminologists have been tackling such issues for many years, it is only recently that economists have entered the arena of controversy. This is not surprising given the high levels of crime and the associated allocation of public and private resources towards crime prevention. The expenditure on the criminal justice system (police, prisons, prosecution/defense and courts) is a significant proportion of government budgets. In addition, firms and households are spending increasingly more on private security.

The incentive-based economic model of crime is a model of decision making in risky situations.

Economists analyse the way in which individual attitudes toward risk affect the extent of illegal behavior. In most of the early literature, the economic models of crime are single-period individual choice models. These models generally see the individual as deciding to allocate time with criminal activity as one possible use of time. A key feature is the notion of utility; judgements are made of the likely gain to be realised (the 'expected utility') from a particular choice of action. Individuals are assumed to be rational decision-makers who engage in either legal or illegal activities according to the expected utility from each activity. An individual's participation in illegal activity is, therefore, explained by the opportunity cost of illegal activity (for example, earnings from legitimate work), factors that influence the
returns to illegal activity (for example, detection and the severity of punishment), and
by tastes and preferences for illegal activity.

Economists see criminal activity as being similar to paid employment in that it
requires time and produces an income. Clearly, the dichotomy between either
criminal activity or legal activity is an oversimplification. For example, individuals
could engage in criminal activities while employed since they have greater
opportunities to commit crime; similarly, some criminals may jointly supplement
work income with crime income in order to satisfy their needs. A secondary problem
with the economist's choice model, which was highlighted in our opening comments,
is that young people are more likely to participate in crime long before they participate in the labor market. This observation raises questions about

the appropriateness of the economic model of crime in explaining juvenile crime.

Economic models of criminal behavior have focused on sanction effects (e.g. deterrence issue) and the relationship between work and crime. In the main, these models have not directly addressed the role of education in offending. It could be argued that unemployment is the conduit through which other factors influence the crime rate. For example, poor educational attainment may be highly correlated with the incidence of crime. However, this may also be a key determinant of unemployment. Although educational variables have been included as covariates with crime rates, they have not received a great deal of attention in correlational studies.

To the basic theory ,economic Model of Criminal Behavior: Basic theory is

as mentioned in the overview, the economic model of crime is a standard model of decision making where individuals choose between criminal activity and legal activity on the basis of the expected utility from those acts. It is assumed that participation in criminal activity is the result of an optimizing individual responding to incentives. Among the factors that influence an individual's decision to engage in criminal activities are (i) the expected gains from crime relative to earnings from legal work (ii) the chance (risk) of being caught and convicted, (iii) the extent of punishment and (iv) the opportunities in legal activities. Specifying an equation to capture the incentives in the criminal decision is a natural first step in most analyses of the crime as work models. The most important of these gives the relative rewards

of legal and illegal activity. For example, the economic model sees the criminal as

committing a crime if the expected gain from criminal activity exceeds the gain from

legal activity, generally work.

Just as in benefit-cost analysis, when comparing alternative strategies, interest

centers on the returns from one decision vis-a-vis returns from another decision. For

example, a preference for crime over work implies the earnings gap between legal

and illegal activities must rise when the probability of being caught and the severity

of punishment increases. Attitudes towards risk are central to economic models of
criminal choice. For example, if the individual is said to dislike risk (i.e., to be risk
averse) then he will respond more to changes in the chances of being apprehended
than to changes in the extent of punishment, other things being equal. Becker
developed a comparative-static model that considered primarily the deterrent effect of
the criminal justice system. As we will see, how individuals respond to deterrent and
incapacitation effects of sanctions has generated considerable theoretical and empirical interest from economists.

Thus, severe sentencing and improvements in legal work opportunities of criminals must be expected jointly to reduce crime. Of course, this assumes that crime and work are determined by the same factors and that higher legitimate earnings increase the
probability of working. In the early literature, economists applied static one period
time allocation models to analyse criminal behavior. In other words, crime and work
are assumed to be substitute activities; if an individual allocates more time to work, he
will commit less crime because he will have less time to do so. The basic economic
model of crime is static or comparative static in economic jargon because it does not
see the potential criminal as considering more than a single time period when making
his decision.

Early studies of criminal behavior by economists can be criticized for being
set in a static framework. Economic models of crime are typically estimated as static
models, though there are many reasons to suspect dynamic effects matter, both
theoretically through habit formation, interdependence of preferences,

capital accumulation, addiction, peer group effects, etc., and empirically through improvements in fit when lagged dependent variables or autocorrelated residuals are included in the model. Labor economists have long been interested in state dependence, the fact that activities chosen in the current period may be strongly affected by the individual's activities in the previous period.

Flinn incorporates human capital formation in a time-allocation model. In his model, human capital is accumulated at work, not at school. Consequently, crime takes time away from work and hence diminishes the amount of human capital accumulated. The diminished human capital leads to lower future wages and hence less time spent working. Since crime and work are substitutes in his model, the decline in time allocated to work leads to increased participation in criminal activities.

In nowadays global labor market, the basic idea underlying the model is that young men have two types of jobs available to them –skilled and unskilled – where wage profiles are rising in the former (due to accumulation of human capital, training and experience) and flat in the latter (no training). If discounted wages are equalized across jobs, the unskilled wage would start above and end below skilled wage. Also, human capital theory suggests that job stability will be greater in skilled sector than in the unskilled sector. Given these predictions, and assuming that a criminal conviction adversely affects prospects of getting a skilled job, it is likely that conviction is associated with higher pay and higher job instability. So, low skillful workers usually do criminal behaviors more than high skillful workers in our societies nowadays.

Concerning how to examine the impact of legitimate labor market experiences (e.g., unemployment) and sanctions on criminal behavior whether they have relationship question? Broadly speaking, the empirical

findings are that (i) poor legitimate labor market opportunities of potential criminals, such as low wages and high rates of unemployment, increases the supply of criminal activities and (ii) sanctions deter crime. Unemployment could be taken to influence the opportunity cost of illegal activity. High rates of unemployment growth could be taken to imply a restriction on the availability of legal activities, and thus serve to ultimately reduce the opportunity cost of engaging in illegal activities. Although theoretically well-defined, most empirical studies of the unemployment-crime relationship have provided mixed
evidence. Instead of primarily focusing on crime as a function of unemployment, they use a richer set of controls, like deterrence, employment status, age, education, race and neighbourhood
characteristics.

One problem with most work and crime models is that they assume both activities are mutually exclusive. This may be a problematic assumption when considering disadvantaged youths. The fact that a youth can shift from crime to an unskilled job and back again or can commit crime while holding a legal job means that the supply of youths to crime will be quite elastic with respect to relative rewards from crime vis-a-vis legal work or to the number of criminal opportunities. From the 1970s through the 1990s the labor market prospects for unskilled workers in most OECD countries has deteriorated considerably. In particular, the real
earnings of young unskilled men fell, while income inequality rose. This suggests that
as the earnings gap widens, relative deprivation increases, which in turn leads to
increases in crime.

A substantial problem that has been ignored in the vast majority of empirical
studies is nonstationarity of crime rates. A time-series is said to be nonstationary if (1)
the mean and/or variance does not remain constant over time and (2) covariance
between observations depends on the time at which they occur. In the US, the index
crime rate appears strongly nonstationary, for the most part being integrated of order
one with both deterministic and stochastic trends (a random variable whose

mean
value and variance are time-dependent is said to follow a stochastic trend) .The empirical results suggest a long-run equilibrium relationship
between crime, prison population, female labor supply and durable consumption.

The explanatory variables include the number of juveniles or adults in custody per crime; the number of juveniles or adults in custody per juvenile or adult; economic variables, including the state unemployment rate and demographic variables, including race and legal drinking age, and dummy variables for year and state. Levitt finds that juvenile crime is negatively related to the severity of penalties, and that juvenile offenders are at least as responsive to sanctions as adults. Interestingly, he finds that the difference between the punishments given to youths and adults helps explain sharp changes in crimes
committed by youths as they reach the age of majority.

Most economic work on crime has focused on the deterrent effect of the criminal justice system and on the interrelationship between work and crime. Empirical work provides some, but not unambiguous support for the deterrence hypothesis. Recent work by economist suggest that the relationship between work and crime may be far more complicated than implied by economic models.

The rise in juvenile crime rates has focused increasing attention on youth crime. This has forced economists to expand their thinking to incorporate such things as education, peer group effects and the influence of family and community. Increasingly both theoretical and empirical work on the economics of crime has come to use dynamic models. Theoretical work is developing multi-period models of crime. Empirically economists are using both panel data techniques and modern time series techniques to examine the dynamics of criminal behavior.

● CRIMINOLOGICAL THEORIES ABOUT
why people commit crime are used—and misused, if poor global economic environment factor was main factor causes people do criminal behaviors?

Every day by legislative policy makers and community corrections managers when
they develop new initiatives, sanctions, and programs; and these theories are also being
applied—and misapplied—by line community corrections officers in the workplace as

they classify, supervise, counsel, and control offenders placed on their caseloads. The
purpose of this article is to provide a brief overview of the major theories of crime causation and then to consider the implications of these criminological theories for current and
future community corrections practice. Four distinct groups of theories will be examined:
classical theories, biological theories, psychological theories, and sociological theories of crime causation. While the assumptions of classical criminology have been used to justify a wide range of sentencing
and corrections policies and practices over the past several decades, it is also possible to identify the influence of other theories of crime causation on corrections policies and practices
during this same period.

As we examine each group of theories, we consider how—and why—the basic functions of probation and parole officers change based on the theory of crime causation under review.
When considering the link between theory and practice, it is important to remember the
following basic truth: Criminologists disagree about both the causes and solutions to our
crime problem. This does not mean that criminologists have little to offer to probation and parole officers in terms of practical advice; to other community corrections programs are to the contrary, we think a discussion of "cause" is be successful as "people changing" agencies. Critical to the ongoing debate over the appro- But can we reasonably expect such diversity priate use of community-based sanctions, and flexibility from community corrections and the development of effective community agencies, or is it more likely that one theory— corrections policies, practices, and programs. or group of theories—will be the dominant.

However, the degree of uncertainty on the influence on community corrections practice?
cause—or causes—of our crime problem in Based on recent reviews of United States
academic community suggests that a rections history, we suspect that one group of
certain degree of skepticism is certainly in theories—supported by a dominant political

order when "new" crime control strategies are ideology—will continue to dominate until
introduced. We need to look carefully at the the challenges to its efficacy move the field—
theory of crime causation on which these new both ideologically and theoretically—in a new
initiatives are based. It is our view that since direction. We may—or may not—be at such a
each group of theories we describe is appli- watershed point in the United States today.

An Overview of Criminological Theories Classically-based criminologists explain criminal behavior as a conscious choice by individuals based on an assessment of the costs and benefits of various forms of criminal activity. Biologically-based criminologists explain criminal behavior as determined—in part—by the presence of certain inherited traits that may increase the likelihood of criminal behavior.

Psychologically-based criminologists explain criminal behavior as the consequence of individual factors, such as negative early childhood experiences and inadequate socialization, that result in criminal thinking patterns and/or incomplete cognitive development.

Sociologically-based criminologists explain criminal behavior as primarily influenced by a
variety of community-level factors that appear to be related—both directly and indirectly—to
the high level of crime in some of our (often poorest) communities, including blocked legitimate opportunity, the existence of subcultural values that support criminal behavior, a breakdown of community-level informal social controls, and an unjust system of criminal laws and criminal justice.

To a classical criminologist, the answer is
simple: The benefits of law breaking (such as money, property, revenge, and status) simply
outweigh the potential costs/consequences of getting caught and convicted. When viewed
from a classical perspective, we are all capable of committing crime in a given situation, but we make a rational decision (to act or desist) based on our analysis of the costs and benefits of the action. If this is true, then it is certainly possible to deter a potential offender by (1) developing a system of

"sentencing" in which the punishment outweighs the (benefit of the) crime, and (2) ensuring both punishment
certainty and celerity through efficient police and court administration. "Classical" theories
of criminal behavior are appealing to criminal justice policy makers, because they are based
on the premise that the key to solving the crime problem is to have a strong system of
formal social control. In other words, the classical theorist believes that the system can make a difference, regardless of the myriad of individual and social ills that exist. During the past four decades, a number of federal, state, and local programs have been initiated to improve the deterrent capacity of the criminal justice system, including proactive police strategies to ensure greater certainty of apprehension,priority prosecution/speedy trial strategies to ensure greater celerity (speed) in the court process, and determinate/mandatory sentencing strategies to ensure greater punishment certainty and severity.

To further our deterrent aims, we have significantly increased our institutional capacity during this same period and passed legislation that includes mandatory minimum periods of incarceration for drug-related crimes, while simultaneously developing a series of surveillance-oriented intermediate sanctions (e.g., intensive probation supervision, electronic monitoring/house arrest) for a subgroup of the offenders under community supervision.

It is apparent from these initiatives that classical assumptions about crime causation are still being used as the basis for current crime control strategies. Some have argued that our four-decade-long emphasis on "deterrencebased"crime control policies has resulted in safer communities; in fact, by most standard measures (crime rates, victimization rates) we have less crime and less violence today than at any point since the early 1970s.

With most experts estimating that about a quarter of the crime decline can be linked to tougher sentencing policies, while three quarters of the decline have been attributed to other factors (such as the economy, education, and immigration). A careful review of the evaluation research indicates that community-based sanctions does not support the notion that increased surveillance and control reduces recidivism (that is, an offender's likelihood of rearrest, reconviction, and/ or re-incarceration). There are two possible explanations for these findings: (1) the underlying assumptions of classical criminologists (i.e., most people are rational, and weigh the costs and benefits of various acts in the same manner) are wrong (e.g., people commit crimes for emotional reasons, because of mental illness, and/or because they believe the criminal act is justified, given circumstances and prevailing community values); or (2) the current sentencing strategies and community corrections programs need to be even tougher and deterrence-oriented (in other words, the theory is correct; it just has not been implemented correctly).

While community corrections populations and probation rates also remain high, and continue to use multiple conditions that emphasize surveillance and control (through drug testing, electronic monitoring, curfews, and now social media monitoring). For example, in the name of deterrence, legislation has been passed in several states allowing the lifetime supervision of paroled. The final group of psychological theories focuses on the potential link between personality and criminality. Although there is currently much debate on whether personality characteristics play a significant role in determining subsequent criminal behavior, a number of prominent criminologists have argued that "the root causes of crime are not...social issues [high unemployment, bad schools] but deeply ingrained features of the human personality and its early experiences. Low intelligence, an impulsive personality, and a lack of empathy for other people are among the leading individual characteristics of people at risk for becoming offenders".

● THE IMPACT OF CRIMINOLOGICAL THEORY WHETHER POOR ECONOMIC ENVIRONMENT IS THE REAL REASON TO INFLUENCE CRIME RATE RAISES

This question concerns to how to implement and the development of

strategies
to assess community "risk" and then relocate offenders who currently reside in "high-risk" neighborhoods to lower-risk areas, utilizing the lure of new job opportunities or housing incentives. A final group of sociological theories of crime causation can be identified, based on the premise that people become criminals not because of some inherent characteristic, personality defect, or other sociologically-based "pressure" or influence, but because of decisions made by those in positions of power in government, especially those in the criminal justice system. The social strategies implementation to reduce crime rate increases may include as below:

Intervention Strategy

(1) Strategies emphasize education, skill development,and employment opportunity.

(2) Strategies emphasize community-level value change, alternatives to gang involvement, and offender relocation.

(3) Strategies target improving community structural conditions, resource availability, and collective efficacy; strengthening informal community social control mechanisms; and eliminating poverty pockets.

(4) Strategies focus on the breakdown of informal social control mechanisms—attachment, commitment, involvement, and belief—and emphasize the importance of the relationship between the offender and his/her probation/parole officer.

(5) Strategies designed to target the turning points in the lifecourse that have been directly related to desistance among adult offenders—marriage, employment, military service, and offender relocation.

(6) Strategies focus on the use of alternative dispute/ conflict resolution strategies that result in lower levels of formal criminal justice system involvement in the lives of

community residents; and on the application of community/ restorative justice principles in traditional criminal justice settings, including community corrections.

All these strategies are supposed that the country's crime rate raises is not due to poor economic environment factor influence mainly. The country's crime rate raising is based on other non economic related factors influence.

Given the potential negative consequences of labeling,we need to ask ourselves: (1) which laws do we really need to enforce? and (2) which offenders can (and should) we divert from the formal court process?

A number of observers have suggested probation and parole officers do not have an adequate "professional base" to do the job we ask them to do. However, it is our view that it is impossible to assess the qualifications of community corrections personnel unless we first clearly define the primary job orientation of the community corrections officer: Do we want our line staff to emphasize treatment or control? As we have indicated throughout this article, how we answer the "why" (or causation) question (Why did the offender commit this crime?) will determine not only our general orientation toward certain categories of crime (e.g., drug offenses, violent crime) and groups of offenders (e.g., sex offenders, gang members, drunk drivers), but also the types of functions we will expect community corrections to perform.

A number of line probation and parole officers only have an undergraduate degree, while some have even less formal education. This diversity in educational background would be a cause for concern if we could clearly establish a relationship between education and the job itself. Unfortunately, we do not have a firm grasp on the types of skills necessary to be an effective probation or parole officer in the next decade. While a number of "get tough" intermediate sanctions programs have been developed based on classical assumptions about crime control (e.g., intensive supervision, house arrest, boot camps), these programs still include only a small percentage (approximately 10 percent) of all offenders under community supervision. If these programs continue to expand, it appears that we will need to draw our POs from the pool of undergraduate criminal justice majors, perhaps requiring some prior experience as a police officer or corrections guard. Such "deskilling" is an inevitable consequence of the movement away from treatment and toward the technology of control.

I shall indicate the developing country, India case example to explain why and how poor economic environment can impact crime rate to be raised in possible as below:

The Economist (2018, pp.7-16) indicated that India Women unemployment rate raised that it had relationship between India poor economic environment and India itself country's unemployment women. It explain as below:

India labour force, women have been falling away at an alarming pace. The female employment rate in India, counting both the formal and informal economy, has raised from an already-low 35% in 2005 to just 26% now. IN that time the economy has more than doubled in size and the number of working-age women has grown by a quarter, to 470 million. Yetnearly 10m fewer womwn are in jobs. A rise in female employment rates to the male level would provide India with an extra 235 m workers, more than the EU has of either geneder,

and more than enough to fill all the factories in the rest in Asia. India has high young female unemnployed number, it may due to many girls need to leave schools to find jobs to do because their families are poor.

However, Economist also indicated other problmes in India nowadays, they include that lacking of employment opportunities.

The workforce has shifted from jobs more often done by women , especially farming, where most Indian women work but are being displaced by mechanisation. At the same time, inflexible and unreformed labour markets have hampered the rise of manufacturing and low-level services, the gateway for women in other poor countries. IN neighhouring Bangladesh, whose customs are not so different from India's. a boom in gament manufacturing has increased the number of working women by 50% since 2005. In Vietnam three-quarters of women work. But the mega-factories that boosted female employment there are largely absent in India.

So, it seems that India's manufacturing industry can not develop successfully, it may due to it lacks confidnece to let overseas or domestic investors to develop any kinds of manufacturing businesses in India as well as India lacks high technological skillful workers number is shortage to supply to India's manufacturing industries in India's labor market. SO, it explains that India's poor economy and low technological manufacturing industry development

and high India female unemployment number, they can bring India's crime rate to be raised in possible.

In fact, India has many male workers who have been encountering unemployment for a long time, instead of India has many young females can not find any jobs to work in India easily. When India has been still encountering the challenge of lacking of enough manufacturing jobs to supply to them to do, instead of farming jobs, this primary industry jobs, e.g. farmers, fruit pickers , cow feeding etc. farming jobs. It can not solve India unemployment challenge. Because

some India high educational young people had graduated in university, but they still feel difficulties to find any suitable jobs to do, it may due to there are less overseas and domestic investors have confidence to set up their businesses in India. SO, high educational jobs are shortage in India.Then, it causes India's economic environment will be become more worse to compare past. So, it seems that India's worse economic enviroment will influence unemploment rises and crime rate rises. I believe that they have direct relationship betweem them.

India's worse economic environment also causes many employees have no preferred the stability of permanent employment mind, they only choose contracted employment or short term , temporary employment in India. They only earn hour paid , or day paid and they feel difficulties to earn monthly paid in India labor market easily.

For India Mc Donald's jobs example, a America fast food company has taken things the furthest, outsourcing 100% of its restaurant jobs, Servers, cooks and cleaners at India McDonald's are no longer employees of the firm or its franchisees, but bid for positions at the till on an hourly basis thtough TaskRabbit, an online labour platform.So, most functions were

completed in-house by permanent, full time employees. Many people worked for only

one or two employers during their careers. That arrangement had been changed by a unreasonable business logic.

It implies that some overseas big company , such as America Mc Donald restaurant also can not provide reasonable welfare to India workers, then they will feel hopeless to earn reasonable wage treatment when they believe that they can work in any one overseas large organizations. In long term, Indian will feel long term unemployment feeling, although, they still have fill time jobs to do because many full time jobs are contract, short term, temporary. So, they need to often to change new employers, even some Indian people working performance are excellent. If Indian working people are luck, they can change another new employers very easily. Otherwise, if they are unluck, then they need to wait short time, e.g. one month or three months, even, they need to wait longer time, e.g. more than six months or more than one year. So, many Indian working people are feeling sudden unemployment occurrence in possible. When their employment contracts are finished ,even if employers decline their offer contract continue. So, if some Indians working people wait need to spend long time to search any jobs, due to jobs are not enough. They will feel unemployment , then crime rate will be influenced to be raised from long time unemployment factor in possible in India nowadays society.

In conclusion, if some countries feel their crime rate raising reason is not caused by poor economic environment factor, they can attempt to apply above strategies to solve crime rating problems to investigate whether poor economic environment factor is the main factor to influence their crime rate raising in possible.

Reference

The Economist, How India Fails its women, July 7 the 2018. pp. 7-16

CHAPTER TWELVE

The relationship between welfare economics and crime rate

I believe that whether the country has better or worse welfare economic environment or its
welfare is improved to satisfy its citizen's living of standard, it will bring effect whether its society's
crime rate is more less. I shall explain why and how the country welfare will influence its crime
rate to be increased or decreased as below reasons:

What does the new welfare economics mean? It can be explained that how the county citizens
interpersonal comparison of utility and social welfare function to their country's welfare policy
to let they feel more satisfactory or less satisfactory. Their satisfaction can include
leisure and non-leisure consumption satisfaction daily. So, if the country can give more welfares to
let its citizen to feel more satisfaction on leisure and consumption aspects. Then, they won't
choose to do any crime activities more easily.

In fact, economists have used no methods of scientific research in arriving at their conclusions
about whether the country can provide better or worse economic welfare, which can influence the
society's crime rate is raised or decreased. However, I shall attempt to explain that why any

country's welfare can let its citizen to satisfy more or less, then it can influence the country's crime rate to be increased or decreased.

Every country's economic welfare was said to be a part of total welfare, as well as it can be brought directly or indirectly into relation with money. Why do some countries change their social welfare, then their crime rate can be improved to reduce really? In other words, a less satisfaction to a man with more money than it will to one with less money. Based on this assumption, when the country has good welfare to provide the low income people, then they will feel more satisfaction on their daily living needs. They won't feel worry their basic foods, living needs. Consequently, the society will increase many low income people , they won't feel difficulty to live, then stealing , fighting etc. opposed social crime behaviors or activities will ought to be decreased, due to the low income people feel or believe their country can feel what they have real essential needs at the moment. The low income people can feel safe to live in the country. Then, the country's crime rate ought to be decreased. So, it seems that crime rate increases or decreases, it has relationship between the country's welfare satisfaction to their essential needs, in specially the low income group.

Why does poor welfare influence the low Income people do crime behaviors more easily? It is simple, for example, when two consumers , they enter the supermarket to make choice to buy apples to eat. When the high income consumer performs to take any good taste apples to buy to eat. The another low income consumer or unemployed consumer , he looks the another consumer is taking any good taste apples to choose which one is the best apple to buy.

During their apply choice process, the low income Or unemployed apple consumer will feel unhappy when he knows the another consumer had chosen the most good taste apples to buy to eat in the supermarket. However, due to the country can not provide the better welfare to support the low income or poor person or unemployed person has enough money to buy any good taste apples to eat in the supermarket. Then, the lacking enough social welfare person , he will do stealing apples crime behavior in the supermarket more easily if he brings one plastic bags. So, if the country has many low income people or poor people or unemployed people are living in the country, they feel that their government can not provide enough welfare to support their essential living need. Then, they will choose to do crime behaviors more easily. Consequently, the country's crime rate will also be raised in possible.

So, I believe that any country's crime rate is more or less, it has relationship to its low income
people whether they feel their country government can give more or less welfare to support their basic daily living needs in order to do any crime behavior more easily. Because one individual's happiness is also , to some extent, dependent on what others consume. Obviously, the standard of living or welfare level of his family is not a matter of indifference to a man. But we do not avoid the difficulty by taking family as a unit. So, when the country has many families are living, if there are many families' fathers , they are not employing or they are often working in the low income level as well as they government can not provide enough welfares to support their living need. It will bring that they feel living pressure to support their children to learn and wife's living need, if their wives are housewives role or without job housewives. So, low income or poor families will do crime behaviors more easily to compare single people, because single people do not need to support their wives and children living cost. So, if the country's families householder group number is more than single householder group number, then the country ought concentrate on supporting more welfare to the householder families group living needs to

reduce their living pressure, e.g. children education assistance, handicapped assistance, low income short time welfare assistance, wife short time unemployed assistance or wife low income assistance. When , they feel lesser living pressure from their government's welfare assistance. Then, these low income families won't do any family fighting or violence or killing themselves families crime behaviors more easily in society.

So, when the country can improved its welfare to be better, then it can encourage many low income people have ability to consume. It will bring its business and economic environment to be better. So, it has case and effect relationship between welfare and economic environment and crime rate to any countries. The most realistic general assumption , we can make is that, when a man saves he is normally saving up to buy a collection similar in composition to that which he is buying when he saves. Therefore, when comparing his welfare for, says, two different years, we must , in effect, scale up his expenditure in the one year until it is equal to his income of that year, and then ask whether, in the other year, he could have bought the scaled-up collection of the one year.

So, every country's government needs to arrange the reasonable welfare to give the different living needs people in itself country. It can ask this question in order to evaluate every low income or poor people's real welfare need, the question is : Could the poor or low income person have bought last year's collection of goods? So, the country government can gather every poor or low income welfare need applicants' past year consumption or purchase price, kinds of product information, e.g. the low income or poor welfare assistance applicant whether he had enough income to buy any electric products , e.g. desktop, laptop computer(s), television, wash machine, fan, air condition etc. home electric products for his family to use last year. If the welfare assistance applicant had any last year electric products purchase record, then I believe that he still have enough income to support his family living, because these are not his basic living need. It means that he ought have enough money to support his family living need in this year. In simple, his welfare assistance ought be less amount to other welfare assistance applicants, they had not bought any home electric products for their families to use last year. So, it is one good evaluation method to assess whether government ought give how much welfare assistance to every welfare assistance applicant in our societies nowadays. Instead, how many number of children number to the families, old age parents are living with or without living to their sons or daughters together, how many children , they are studying primary, secondary or university etc. families member living dependence factor will also need to be considered to assess every family welfare assistance needs. However, it is reasonable that when the family has many lacking independent ability of members who are living together, then this family ought be provided more welfare assistance need to compare the family has many independent ability of members who are living together, because when family has many independent members are living together, they must have more income source to compare the family has less independent members are living members are living together. It means that the family total income must be enough to support whose living need more easily to compare the less number independent family member case.

Thus, welfare economics and ethics can not then , be separated. They are inseparable because the welfare is a value terminology. The answer is that it could be such a system was held to be anything, for example, welfare or happiness, it would once again be emotive and ethical. The subject is one about which nothing interesting can be said without value judgements, for the reason that every country government needs take a moral interest in welfare and happiness to let it poor people or low income people feel less living pressure, when they can feel their government is really considerate their living needs. Also if we propose to use a certain criterion for an increase the economic welfare of an individual, then the country ought can raise the poor or low income people's consumption ability or consumption desires. Consequently, when their consumption behaviors are encouraged to raise any kinds of products are sold easily from them. The country's economy will be improved to be better. Then, the stealing crime cases will also cause to be decreased directly.

In conclusion, I believe that these above cases can explain that why it have direct relationship between welfare economy and consumer behavior and crime rate. Every country government ought considerate how to arrange the reasonable welfare level to satisfy the different real welfare need applicants' real living needs in order to avoid unfair welfare assistance treatment to let every welfare assistance applicant feel unfair and angry to themselves country government. Thus, welfare economy has real relationship to influence every country's consumer behaviors or consumption desires to be increase or decrease as well as their crime behavioral causation.

www.ingramcontent.com/pod-product-compliance
Ingram Content Group UK Ltd.
Pitfield, Milton Keynes, MK11 3LW, UK
UKHW021923190726
13853UKWH00002B/813